HOW TO GET ON THE EMPLOYMENT LADDER

You have the skills; now learn to DEVELOP them

Tracey Morewood©

Published by Tracey Morewood 2012

Copyright © Tracey Morewood

For those that say you can't
I am telling you, you can.

Follow the steps inside this book
to reach your full potential and gain employment.

Contents

Praise

I would like to share with you all some of the comments I have had from people who I have helped gain employment. And like the subtitle of this book suggests; you have the skills, now learn to develop them. To which these lovely people did.

"Well one thing I did learn from you Tracey is there is no such word as fail. Without your help I can tell you I know I wouldn't be going in April to work in Spain as a childcare rep. You gave me so much inspiration it's unreal Tracey!"

"You've opened up a whole new path for me and laid down the groundwork. I am so grateful for every little thing you did for me."

Lee Crouch, Leeds. Employed Overseas Childcare Rep.

"When I first met Tracey I was a very self conscious person who lacked self belief. Tracey and the book helped me come out of myself and it was drilled it into me that I can do anything that I put my mind to! I always knew that if I needed extra support and guidance, Tracey would be there for me. It gave me so much faith to know that what I was saying wasn't stupid and that I was just as good as anybody else. Tracey is a fantastic teacher. All the help and belief that she had in me helped me succeed in getting my new job! To this day I still think about the fantastic advice that Tracey has given me, I hear her voice in my head saying; "You can do this Emma, you can do anything you put your mind to."

There are no words to explain how much Tracey and her book has helped me. I have a fantastic future ahead of me all thanks to Tracey and the book."

Emma Barraclough, Otley. Employed Childcare Rep.

*"The book offered encouragement and guidance and it has helped increase my self-belief and confidence. I previously **thought** I had employable skills - now I **know** I have. The book showed me how to keep my determination and motivation on a daily basis. Constantly inspiring faith and belief.*

I feel I gained the following through reading the book:

1. *Encouragement and guidance in my search to find employment.*
2. *Increased my self-belief and confidence.*
3. *Increased my belief in my skills and abilities.*
4. *Helped to increase my determination and motivation to find employment.*
5. *Fantastic interview skills, no matter what type of interview I attend."*

Jo Mills, Pontefract, Employed Cleaner

"I just wanted to let you know that my new job is going great and it's all thanks to you. I would never have stood a chance of getting a permanent job at my age (51) without all the great advice and encouragement that I received from you. You gave me a belief that I was still employable. You taught me to be confident and to believe I was the best candidate for the job and I achieved that through all your hard work. Many people who cross your path will find work through your great teaching and relaxed approach. I am forever in your debt, God bless you."

Gary Chambers, West Yorkshire, Employed Team Leader

The first time I met Tracey was when I was interviewing for a new Employability Coach. I had seen several potential candidates before Tracey, all perfectly qualified to do the role, but none of them came in with the enthusiasm and determination that she brought into the room. After the interview had finished I knew I had found my new coach.

Since then I have watched as Tracey has taken groups of people with low self-esteem and little belief in themselves and through her down to earth and honest approach, mentor people back into the employment market.

What Tracey does so well is to allow people to gain belief in themselves and to make their own decisions to move forward, to understand what skills they already possess, to be honest with themselves, and decide in what direction they need to be going. The feedback I have got from clients for the help they had received has been both excellent and positive, but more importantly the clients now felt this way about themselves.

This book gives the reader the opportunity to develop the skills they need, not just to get a job but also to have the faith in their own abilities to do it well and to progress in their chosen career.

As I have often heard people tell Tracey when they first meet her, *"I've been on other courses and nothing has worked"*. To which her reply is *"You haven't met me yet."* I can honestly say I've met Tracey and what she delivers does work, and works well.

Ian Harrison, Employability Co-ordinator

I have worked alongside a variety of people who were good at their job but didn't get the desired results and didn't feel the passion that I did.

Tracey however has an unrivalled passion, enthusiasm and dedication to the delivery of employment skills. Her ideas and the way she motivates and inspires the people she teaches is inspirational and amazing to watch. **People listen**! She takes a no-nonsense and honest approach to the passing on of the skills they will need to help them compete in the job market.

It works, and is relevant to the learners and taught in a language they can understand and identify with. People she has taught are moving into employment and leave with the confidence and belief that they can do anything.

Gina Waite, Employability Tutor

My Sincere Thanks

There are quite a few people who I would like to thank within this book. The first are my two boys Ellis and Connor, for screaming, arguing and falling out all the way through it. But you have both being very supportive and I love you more than words can say. I am so proud of you, you are amazing children. Thank you mum and dad for all of your support. Love you so much. Big sis, you encourage me and believe in me so much. Thank you.

Another person whom I would like to thank is Mr 'B', who always said that there is a book within me, he taught me to look for something I was passionate about. He said that once I had found that passion the rest would be easy. Thank you for all of your guidance, help and reassurance.

Which brings me onto my passion, my learners; whether it is within Offender Learning or within the Employability Sector. For those that I have taught, thank you. You will probably never realise the motivation and passion you have given me. You have all made me realise that not everything is *black* and *white*. There is usually a deeper meaning to why we feel how we often do. Without meeting many of you I would never have experienced or found my passion for educating others. I would never have realised that I can actually make a difference to peoples' lives and inspire others. Thank you all from the bottom of my heart.

Gina and Ian you listened to my ideas, you took on board my views and opinions and let me run with what I thought was best. You gave me the motivation through your words of praise of how I have helped get people back into work through my own hard work, passion and dedication.

To you, my reader. Put your trust in this book and me and you will go a long way. I can only promise you that if you take my advice you will start to see a difference with your employment status. I fully believe that to educate, the educator should first have the passion and secondly, they should actually know what they're talking about.

I have both, and I will share all of my knowledge with you about changing your employment status.

Thank you to all of my Facebook friends and previous learners for giving me your opinion and views for the title.

Lastly, Bruno. Without you none of this would be possible, *'everything happens for a reason.'* You have been my rock and best friend throughout this; I am so inspired by you. I always knew you were a crusty loaf: hard on the outside, but all soft and fluffy on the inside.

WHY SHOULD YOU READ THIS BOOK?

This book takes you through a *'process'*, from beginning to end. From creating your C.V to being able to sit in front of an interviewer. Sounds easy? It will be once you have read through all of the sections. But what I do is different. I display my passion and enthusiasm within each session I teach. Oh, and I actually know a lot about this. I actually teach this process every day so I know the impact and the importance of getting it right and standing out from the crowd. And my learners certainly do stand out from the crowd, or at least those who want to. I have made a difference, and I will make a difference to you too. My career experiences range from manager to warehouse operative, from shop assistant to teacher. I have recruited, interviewed, read through CVs etc and like I said earlier, I teach this every day.

You should read this book if you want to know the following:

- How to become employable by displaying *'social skills'*
- How to get the best from your C.V
- How to tailor your C.V
- How not to do your C.V
- How to *'back up'* your C.V
- How to develop your 'soft skills'
- How to overcome your barriers
- How to change your thinking process slightly
- How to appear confident, even though you may be *'bricking'* it.
- How to use the speculative approach
- How to use the *star* approach
- How to use effective communication
- How you can stop yourself being filtered as *'unemployable'*
- How to sail through an interview regardless of the type of interview being held.
- **How to get a job and become employable**

Do you still need persuading? Of course you do, basically each section of this book is broken down into steps. Each step focuses on one main topic.

1

This topic is then broken down even further, and then even further. So you will understand why you are doing something and how it can benefit you. I will tell you how you can get that job, and how easy it will become. You have the skills, I am just going to help you see those skills and give you extra knowledge along the way on how to utilise them to your advantage.

WHO SHOULD READ THIS BOOK?

This book is aimed at people who are out of work, facing redundancy, wanting to improve on their job prospects and those who are wanting to change careers.

I don't care whether you have been out of work for years. I can help you. I guarantee that, although I cannot get you the job (you will be doing that quite easily) you certainly will have every bit of knowledge needed to move forward. I understand that the prospect of going for that promotion or changing your career is a daunting task, I have been there, but you can do it. I will guide you and support you every step of the way. Every part of this book is from my own knowledge and experience. Every example I give is from the learners' experience and my own. No bull, just straight to the point. I know there is other information out there, but throughout this book I break it down into smaller chunks. I will explain the 'why's' the 'how's' and the 'not's'. Because like I have said, I do this every day. I have been in education for a number of years so I have the experience and knowledge to help you succeed.

But my main point I want to share is that I left school with no qualifications. I often say that all I left school with is a bottle of cider. I had no interest in education; I couldn't wait to leave school.
I have been *de-motivated* and had to put up with frequent *put downs* and lacked *self-belief and confidence* too. So I feel that I can relate to almost every one of you.
This book is all from experience and knowledge; I've not just read some stuff on the web then copied and pasted it.

2

WHO SHOULD NOT READ THIS BOOK?

Of course there are people who I would not recommend this book to:

- Those who love academically written articles and books
- Those who just want to copy out a C.V

Well that's not a long list really. But the reason they are there is because:

1. This book is written how I speak. No big words to impress you. No jargon that makes me look intelligent. You may even find the odd mistake; the grammar will probably make some people angry, so what. The message is still there, my aim is still there. So if you want to know the secret to getting a job or changing career and going for promotion then thank you and well done for choosing this book. You won't be let down.

2. You will soon realise that only *you* can create your perfect C.V. Although you will still learn something new from the C.V steps, it will actually be you that creates it. The reason will become much clearer as you read the book.

HOW TO USE THIS BOOK

I recommend that you read through every part of this book, even though you may think that some steps are of no use to you. They will be, honest. Once you have read the book, you will have already gained a wealth of information; you will then need to practice using this information.

I have written this book in sections, each one of these sections is a step with **aims** and **objectives**. If you need to, just focus on one step at one time then fine. At the end of each step I have given you a summary (to remind you) of what you have just done. Also I have added a '*notes page*', here you can write down any particular notes of importance (although it is all important), or reminders of what to take into consideration.

3

I will say again that every part of this book is important, but don't rush through it. I want you to only move on when you feel that you have taken in the knowledge I have just given you.

ONE LAST IMPORTANT SELLING POINT
(SHOULD YOU NEED IT)

On average I have seen learners over a two week period, and in that time from start to finish not one person has finished their learning journey without taking something from me (and I don't mean my purse). Hand on heart I guarantee you that I have helped every learner I have come in contact with. Yes even from those learners who openly admit that they thought they *knew everything*. I guarantee you that when you have read this book you will have skills for life, to transfer from job to job and career to career. I will keep mentioning the fact that this book is made from *'hands on experience'*, and from my own knowledge on the subject.

People have gained employment and/or positive employability skills due to:

- Intensive interview preparation
- Gaining confidence and realising they are just as good as the next person
- Believing in themselves
- Understanding their *hidden skills* (like you will)
- Realising how valuable their C.V is
- Developing their understanding of the importance of communication
- Knowing how to adapt their C.Vs and spec letters to fit the job description
- Being self aware and being proud that they have got something to offer
- Knowing how to job search correctly

And the reason I have outstanding results is:

4

"I have the passion, enthusiasm and determination to help people realise their potential, regardless of their personal situation."

Everything and more you will learn throughout this book.

WHAT BENEFITS ARE THERE TO READING THIS BOOK?

Believe me that you will benefit immensely from reading this book, especially if you want to get back into work or go for promotion. People who have been in this type of profession a lot longer than I have will often come to me for advice. Why?

Because I have a successful track record of helping people get back into work and I teach with passion and enthusiasm and believe that you can get that job; you just need to work a bit harder on some of the skills I will teach you.

People who I have taught have said to me that they have been on other courses similar to what I have taught on; they then say, "*What makes this so different?*" My reply is always the same, "*You've not met me yet!*"

Throughout this book I will take you on the most important journey of your life. I will take you through a process; this process is the key to gaining employment/promotion and to changing careers. This book is your own personal process.

UNDERSTANDING THE EMPLOYMENT FILTER

You will hear me mention the word *filter* throughout this book. But you really must take my advice and get to know the filtering system (also covered later). Throughout your job search process, at each stage you will be filtered in the minds of the interviewer/employer.

My aim is to make it really hard to get filtered under the negative process. Remember it's an employer's market out there; they have the best pick of some excellent skilled people.

THE PROCESS AND JOURNEY AHEAD

Below I have listed how you will get to the end goal of getting a job and/or going for that promotion or career change.

As I mentioned on the back of the book, there is a great big chunk of information missing regards getting on the employment ladder. The journey you are about to start covers every single thing needed to gain employment.

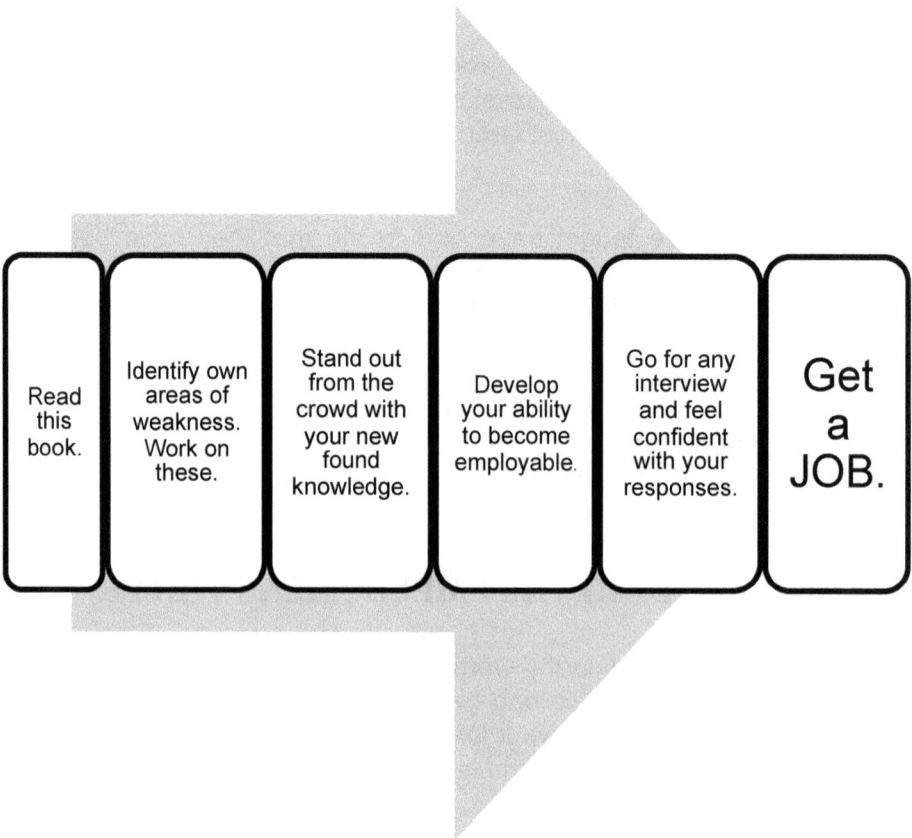

| Read this book. | Identify own areas of weakness. Work on these. | Stand out from the crowd with your new found knowledge. | Develop your ability to become employable. | Go for any interview and feel confident with your responses. | Get a JOB. |

THE AIM OF THIS BOOK

To get a job and/or to gain the confidence to go for that promotion or career change. I can't use big words or phrases to emphasise this aim. To get a job and to become what is known as:

"Being Seen as Employable"

"To assist you and support you if you are wanting a chance to get on the employment ladder. If you are thinking of a career change and/or progression within an existing company."

That is the aim!

I don't care if you have been on training courses, bought other books or researched the internet; I am going to go deeper into how you can help yourself gain employment. This comes from experience. Because you will, I promise you, you will stand out from the crowd and gain employment. Basically, throughout this book I will give you the tools you will need to gain employment, change careers and/or progress. I will show you that gaining employment is not just about creating a good C.V. It is about gaining '*employable*' skills. Creating an excellent C.V is vital, but it's only part of the process.

My main aim is to get you sat before an interviewer feeling confident with the skills you already have. Yes, you already have these skills you just don't realise it. You will though, this is certain. You need to go through the process, you can't rely on luck.

ALREADY IN WORK, BUT WANT TO MOVE ON AND PROGRESS

This book will also give those who are seeking to further their career or even change careers a great amount of fantastic knowledge and the skills to do so. Skills learnt throughout this book are *skills for life*, not just for the next impending interview or just to get your C.V up to scratch. You will realise that these skills will help you throughout life.

7

These skills I am talking about are what are missing from a lot of people, whether in employment or not. There is a reason why the unemployment figures are rising, and to me these are just a few of them; a lack of *employable* skills, and more importantly a lack in *self-confidence, communication* and *self-belief;* without communication skills, self belief and confidence you won't get far. I am not going to sugar coat things and within this book you will realise that I speak and write from experience and every single example is from true life events.

Why do so many people feel that they cannot progress within their existing company or make that career change? Many have a lack of self-confidence and self belief.

From beginning to end, I will explain in detail, give examples and supply you with enough knowledge and confidence to make you **stand out** from the crowd.

Look at the acknowledgements at the beginning of the book, these people have made an impact on me because they took on board everything I said; and, for many gained employment or progression. For those that didn't gain employment straight away have all felt and said the following (or something similar):

"I really didn't think that I would ever feel employable again, but because of you and what you have taught me I fully believe that I will get a job because I believe in myself. Something I haven't done for a long time."

Before I go onto the steps it is really important to give you an overview of why these skills are important. Without them you are not going to get very far in life. So just bare with me (I don't mean to go on), but this overview and knowledge is vital.

Remember:

"Knowledge is powerful, be powerful with this knowledge"

Tracey Morewood

8

INTRODUCTION AND STATISTICS

We all know about the doom and gloom of the job crisis we are facing in Britain, and it is not going to get better any time soon. But, there are jobs out there. Yes there are. The key is to mould yourself into one of those positions you see advertised at the Job Centre, in the Local Weekly Newspaper or Internet. This may sound hard to do, but believe me, through this book I will help you to stand out from the crowd and become employable.

As I write this book, the Government statistics show that the unemployment crisis has now risen by 48,000 to 2.67 million in the three months to December 2011(*http://www.bbc.co.uk/news/10604117*). So the need to 'stand out' is even more important.

As mentioned earlier, this book will also give you the tools, knowledge and confidence to go for that promotion and the skills you may need to change your career. Trust me. By the time you have read this book you will have gained a great amount of knowledge. You will have enough knowledge and confidence to get out there and secure a job, you will have the self belief to go for that promotion and/or change your careers.

WHAT DO I MEAN BY 'EMPLOYABILITY SKILLS'?

These are skills needed to gain employment, gain promotion and even change careers. There is no set criteria of people who may need help with some sort of employability skill. Every one of us has a barrier, yes, even those 'high flyers', your line manager or any other person. It is this barrier that stops us from progressing. I will go more into this throughout the book.

Whether it's your C.V, nerves at an interview or even the thought of 'selling your skills' to the interviewer, this book will help anyone who is either unemployed or employed and wanting to change career or progress further within their existing company.

9

The main and often under-estimated employability skill is the use of communication and soft skills (more later). This doesn't mean just speaking to somebody, from the way in which you speak (tone) to the way in which you walk are all communication skills that many of us lack. And it is this skill that nearly all employers want, you being able to communicate. I will break this down further and explain each part of communication within one of these sessions. There is more to communication than just talking.

THE BEGINNING OF YOUR JOURNEY

I mentioned at the very beginning of the book that to gain the employable skills many employers want; we first need to go through a *process*. It is at this stage I would say to my learners, *"I am this process."* I tell them truthfully that if they want to change, then to listen and learn from what I say. I promise them that they will complete the course with a whole range of skills and knowledge to be able to 'stand out'. To date, not one person who has completed the course told me that they have wasted their time, or that they have not learnt anything.

Example:

On the first day of a new course a group of learners looked fed up. After all, many of them had been on similar course with other training providers. But one thing that they had not come across yet was one vital tool to gaining employability skills.

ME

Loud mouth Yorkshire lass, with a massive passion for helping others achieve their potential.

After 2 hours the whole group had informed me that they had taken so much from the lesson.

10

To gain employment or promotion you will need to go through this process. Sadly, the time of just knowing somebody is not good enough to get you into employment. This book takes you through all of the processes, giving examples from true events and getting you ready to face the interviewer. How do I know this book can help? Because I am an employability tutor. And a good one at that. I know how to get the best out of everybody, and more importantly I know how to get you employable.

I will say this again, I have found my *passion*, and at long last I actually believe in myself. Throughout my teaching years I can always relate to a situation, either I have been there myself or I know somebody that has. Can you see how confident I am? I wasn't always like this, as you are about to find out. But read this book and you will gain new skills and certainly lots of knowledge.

BREAKING DOWN YOUR BARRIERS

DISCOVER YOUR BARRIER AND WORK ON IT

Whether you like it or not, we all have barriers. We are all stuck in our own *'comfort zone'*. Even confident, successful people all have barriers; believe me I have supported a wide range of learner and some intelligent professional people.

Throughout the book I will be helping you break down your barriers and recognise areas in which you need to focus more on. Ask yourself the following:

- What is stopping you from going for that promotion?
- What is stopping you from changing your career?
- What is stopping you from gaining employment?

Most of the time, the answer to the above questions is simply **you.**

By the time you get to the end of the book, I guarantee you that you will have gained knowledge and skills that can be used for life. Look at the opportunity's you could miss because of the bloody *comfort zone*.

I will go further into coming out of your *comfort zone* and breaking down your own *personal barriers* later on within the book.

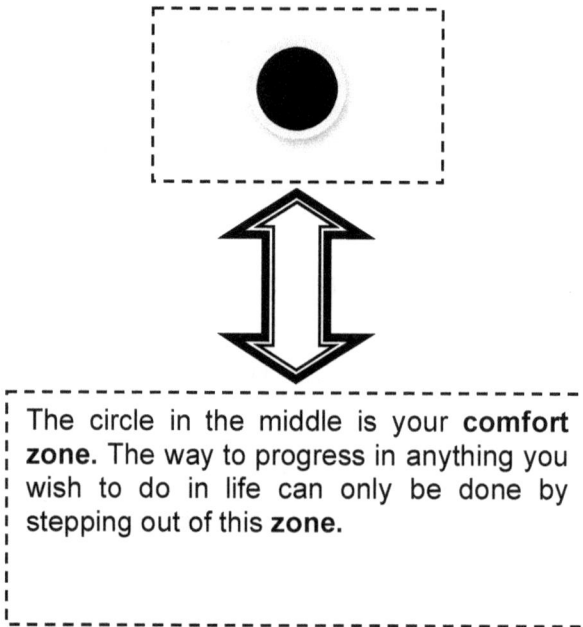

The circle in the middle is your **comfort zone**. The way to progress in anything you wish to do in life can only be done by stepping out of this **zone**.

YOU ARE BEING FILTERED AT EACH STEP

Throughout this book you will hear me mention about the *filtering system*. Basically you are being filtered out within each step of the employment process. Within seven seconds you are being judged as you arrive to the interview.

What I want to do is to give you the knowledge and guidance to help you develop your skills to stop you being filtered out of the exit door. Follow the tips within the book and you will see the interview floodgates start to open. I must warn you though; you will have the skills, now work your backsides off to develop them!

Imagine the illustration below is a filter of information. This information is all about you and rightly or wrongly you will be judged all the way throughout the job seeking process. Make sure you are filtered correctly. At what stage does the filter start? You are being filtered from your first phone call for the application form or from the employer seeing your cover letter. Very early on without realising it, this is when you are being filtered.

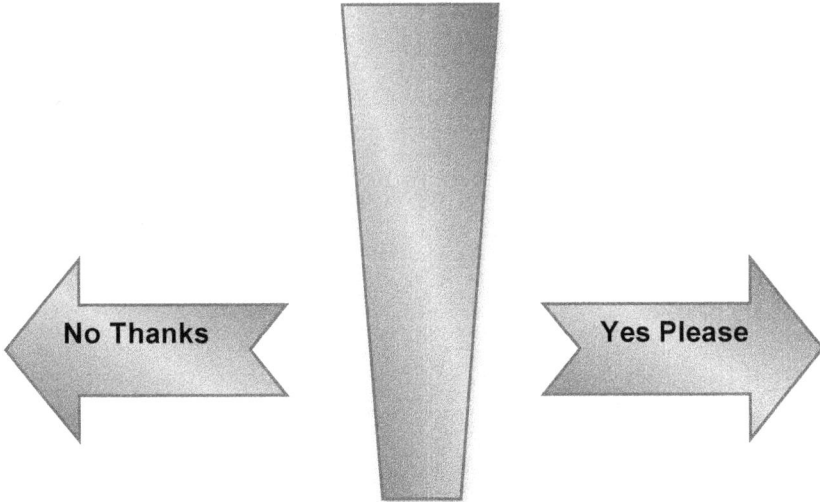

No Thanks

Yes Please

DEVELOPING YOUR "SOFT SKILLS"

HOW TO GET THESE SKILLS FOR FREE

What are soft skills? Basically, soft skills are skills which we all possess but don't often display them. I have worked on building soft skills throughout all of my teaching years. These have often been under estimated by employers and learners, but let me tell you, these skills are going to play a key part in securing that job. I have always thought that these skills have been undervalued, and now employers are starting to realise this too. Employers now feel that these skills can sometimes carry more importance than qualifications. Through much research into what employers look for, soft skills rates highly at the top.

No longer overlooked by qualification after qualification, highlighting your ability to demonstrate and use soft skills will stand you in a more prominent position when going for the interview and applying for jobs.

Soft skills can consist of the following:

- Effective communication
- Team player
- Self confidence and self belief
- Good work ethic
- Interpersonal skills
- People skills
- Problems solving
- Negotiation
- Time management
- Transferrable skills
- Sociability
- Empathy and understanding
- Considerate

Soft Skills continued:

15

- Common sense
- Positive attitudes
- Responsible
- Integrity
- Flexible and adaptable

One common mistake is that most people think that to gain *"employability skills"* the individual first needs to be out of a job. Wrong.

Employability skills affect everyone, even those who are already working at the moment, me included. Employers often feel that these skills can improve businesses and create a high moral of staff which apparently makes a great place to work.

MY RANT AT THE GOVERNMENT

As you can see the list of soft skills is quite long, but we all have these qualities and skills, it may be that we need to dig about to find them within ourselves. Throughout this book I will have given you the tools to look inside yourself and promote these within every aspect of your journey to gaining employment or switching jobs.

Let me tell you, each time I watch the news about un-employed people and the statistics I feel like shouting at the T.V:

"You're doing it wrong, don't just push them onto a course which focuses on job searching, this is not the answer. How are they being taught? Are the tutors getting enough support to help the learner? Are the tutors well informed about the subject? Don't just see these people as lazy, get down to the basics and rebuild their confidence and self belief. You will get more positive results in treating everyone as an individual and knowing that each individual has a different barrier to overcome."

Listen to the news and you will see that it is looking bleak for the 16 – 24 year old category. Again, they have lost their confidence in themselves and in our economy. They cannot gain *work experience*, unless they are placed on it from certain providers or the Job Centre. This is having a knock on effect on their confidence which links to: motivation, self belief etc. Speaking to many of these people, they often feel worthless and that there is just no point in trying to get a job because they are just going to be *rejected.* Depression is one of the health issues I have come across over the years, and deters the individual from finding the confidence to *get out there* and make a difference. Are they depressed because of the economy? Who knows, but it certainly won't be helping them.

Yes, I agree with the programmes in place as it infuriates me that people are beating the system.

Believe me when I say that I have had many people tell me that they do not want a job, they want to stay in the luxury they have got used to.

17

They want to live of the state for ever. These are the people that should be made to earn their money. But, there are also a lot of people who are working their backsides off to gain employment. But again, they could be pushed onto another course going round and around the system. Completing new C.V after C.V (not always good ones either) without focusing on the hidden skills that employers really do value. So rather than blaming everyone else for the high statistics of unemployment, do something different.

Each week I would normally interview around 20 people to see if they are suitable for the course I work on. So many times I have had tears in my eyes; this is because many of them need help. Somebody to listen to their worries or concerns. To tell them that they are actually a worthwhile person.

"Develop a person's soft skill and their self belief first. The rest will then just follow. Give them a chance to even be aware of where they need to develop."

Tracey Morewood

BREAK THROUGH THE BARRIERS

The most important thing I have brought into any of my classes has been the ability to break down barriers to learning and building self confidence. We all have these barriers, I know I do and I will work on these each day. These barriers could be anything from lacking confidence; negative thoughts and doubting own ability. One of my own barriers is *driving* to places I am not familiar with. Honest, the thought scares me.

To overcome this (after I split with the ex husband) I bought a *Sat Nav*. My next barrier to overcome is actually using it! I am getting there slowly, step by step. If I ever mention (and I will) positivity and motivation, then please don't think I am lecturing or preaching to you. I am not. I don't do preaching. But a key skill is having positivity and motivation, especially when you are in an interview (more later). In the examples given throughout the book, I will explain what these individuals gained from the skills I have taught them.

18

CHANGING CAREERS OR WANTING PROMOTION

Throughout this book all of the skills and knowledge I will help you get, are not just to gain employment. No, they can be transferred to change your career and/or go for promotion. These skills are still necessary to do this, but you can do it. Believe me I am talking from experience. Break through your barriers, whatever yours are but do this step by step. There will always be that one person who will try to plant a seed of doubt in your mind about your choices. Don't let them, they are jealous. If you really want something, then work hard and you will get it. A lot of people will give you their negative view, so what. It only gets to be a problem if you listen.

"Dip your toe out of your comfort zone and soon you'll be dive bombing through your barriers. If you stay where you are because of your barriers you will never get to taste opportunity."

Tracey Morewood

The bottom line here is: Don't be scared, see things as new experiences you have not yet gone through. I will go more into that later.

COMMON BARRIERS

So what is one of the main barriers I have seen within my learners? Confidence, well more to the point, the lack of confidence. Many successful people also lack confidence within the workplace; a lot will just wear a mask to cover it up. How do I know? Because I am (or was) one of those people. I too doubted that I could carry out certain tasks. I doubted my own skills. But I won't anymore. I really do practice what I preach, (well most of the time).

How many people do you see in ordinary everyday situations and you think to yourself, "I wish I had their confidence." Well, let me tell you a secret, not all of them are really that confident. They are in their own comfort zone, but take them out of that and their confidence slips. But here's a question; why shouldn't you be successful.

19

There is nothing you can say to me to convince me that you don't deserve success, within this book I hope to give you more confidence in believing in yourself and going for that job, promotion or career change.

So how come a lot of people still want and need to gain employability skills, but have no idea where to get them? How come a lot of people still don't understand how important these skills are to get people prepared for work? Yes, it frustrates the hell out of me too. Knowing I can help a lot people, but these people don't realise this help is there. Well it is now!

But what I will always say to my learners' is this:

*"**Take ownership and be responsible, don't just wait for somebody to come along and give you these skills, get out there and help yourself.**"*

Now let's carry on.

PROGRESSION WITHIN YOUR COMPANY

As mentioned earlier, employability skills are not just for the un-employed. They are for anyone who is looking to either gain employment, further their career within their existing company or looking for a change of career.

I have given advice to many people about how to set up their C.V, how to prepare for interviews, how to back up their C.V using the STAR method and many other skills. Look at how many companies invest in their own staff. How many promotions have you seen within your own organisation which you doubt you have the skills to go for the job? I have also been in that situation, doubted that I could do a certain job, didn't have the confidence to apply for fear of rejection or for fear of looking stupid.

But I always keep telling myself; "*I am the only person holding me back; I am just as good as anyone else.*"

A simple yet meaningful statement, which I need to keep repeating each day. For those of you who are out of work or even in work and wishing to progress. Are you familiar with the word *rejection*? Yes, I bet you are.

Who likes being rejected? I would imagine that nobody does, the rejection letters from employers leads to a lack of confidence, self belief and negativity. I have also witnessed this first hand.

Rejection and the fear of it doesn't always come from '*not getting the job*'. In my experience this fear has been with the individual most of their life and quite often they don't know how to move on from it. Many people have been '*put down*' most of their life, so they feel that they don't deserve better.

Sadly, this links so much to un-employment or stuck in a system or job which you see no future. You may have been brought up with your own parents on benefits, take control of your own life and use the skills and knowledge within this book to make a difference.

21

Self-believe and confidence can be a huge turning point in your life. Again, don't worry you will get there. Read this book carefully and I promise you, it will help.

MY TEACHING STYLE

I have been in teaching for just over 6 years, leaving school with nothing - no qualifications to speak of. But let me tell you, I believe in what I do. I teach with passion and care about my learners. I believe that passion should be in all educators, sadly it isn't! I have a great deal of life experience and a lot more qualifications than when I first left school.

But, please don't be under any illusion that this book will be full of big words and academically written. Yes, I have gained a great deal more qualifications as previously mentioned but I am still a down to earth Yorkshire girl with a caring nature towards helping others (which, to me overtakes the Grammar Cops any day). To which I feel I owe a lot of success, I have enjoyed every part of the learners' journey. I am a big believer in that I would never give my learners anything to do *"just for the sake of it,"* or to *"get bums on seats"*, there has got to be a meaning to every part of my sessions, an aim and an objective that all learners can clearly see and learn from. Each activity within this book is linked to employability, I will explain in more detail as you go through the book. Throughout this book I am going to take you through every step you need to prepare for that all important interview, from beginning to end. So when you find yourself in front of the interviewer/s you will have the skills, knowledge and tools needed to help you gain employment, change career or go for that promotion.

So the question is, are you ready for employment, change of career or promotion and progression within your existing company?

Well, after reading this book you certainly will be.

EXAMPLE OF SUCCESS

Whilst working with a small group of people, each one had their own barrier, mainly a lack of confidence and self belief. One person in particular stood out from the rest as she was really lacking in self belief, confidence and own ability to *'do anything good'* (as her parents had drummed into her). After two weeks she had her interview and I got a lovely text message saying. *"You have done it, you have helped me so much and you have changed my life, I have been offered the job."*

I cried. As I usually do. I often shed a tear because somebody or something will happen each day, I always take a positive from each of my sessions and this was it. I told her I just gave her the tools and support but the rest was down to her. This shy, negative person stood in front of her interviewers and gave a two minute presentation. Something she vowed she would never ever have the courage to do beforehand.

So what about the others who didn't get offered a job? Let me tell you, they may not have got the job, but after two weeks of teaching them the same skills **you** are going to get through this book was unbelievable. But the biggest thing was, they each text me to say that they will get another job; they will not be just another statistic. They all believed that they had the necessary skills and abilities to gain employment. You may think that I failed these learners. But what they have taken is a skill which they didn't realise they had. They have the *soft skills* and the *confidence* to transfer their knowledge to any part of their life; within employment or in day to day living.

To this day these learners still keep in touch to tell me that life won't beat them to tell me that they are either in employment or have decided to go back to college to gain further qualifications. Each one of these learners would always say only positive things about the way in which they have gained their knowledge.

23

Example of success

One man had worked all of his life and he had just been made redundant. He had never needed a C.V, or to work on his confidence and communication skills. An interview for this individual in the past was a handshake or a pint with somebody who knew somebody, who knew somebody. No formal interview or impressive C.V was needed.

But, the job offers where not coming in. Nobody wanted to interview him. Why? Times had certainly changed. He spoke to somebody at the JCP (Job Centre Plus), and they referred him onto the training programme I work for. After his initial induction and assessment he was ready to start. First of all I looked at his C.V, again, not good enough. I then sat with him and asked him questions about what he had done within his career. This is an important part of C.V building (more on that later). With the information he gave me, we re-created his C.V. He was in a much stronger position to send it off with confidence. The next step was communication techniques and then interview skills. Towards the end of the programme he mentioned that he had an interview. We went through possible questions and what he should and should not do.

The outcome:

Within his interview he came 2nd out of 96 people. Another job was coming up in the next few weeks and the interviewer told him that they were so impressed with his C.V and interview skills that they would like to keep him on file and put him forward for the vacancy which was coming up.

This individual text me as I was travelling home from work on the train. Yes, you've guessed it, the tears started. Especially when he said:

"I thank you so much Tracey. I had no idea how hard it was to become employable, but with your skills you have helped, even in areas I didn't realise I needed help with. I have the knowledge and tools to go to any interview because of your in depth interview techniques, support and advice." There have been so many different stories and positive feedback from learners it is impossible to put them all down in this book. But even listening to someone can help them put their life back on track. Quite often I have been a shoulder to lean on.

WHAT TYPE OF PEOPLE HAVE I HELPED?

During my time as an employability tutor I have had the pleasure of helping a variety of people gain employment and to gain the confidence to attend interviews with confidence. But not only do I do this as my job, I often get people phoning, emailing etc to ask certain questions or to help fill in their application form.

The learners who I help do not all fit into the category of the stereo-typical unemployed individual. Sadly, some do. Those who do not wish to find work won't benefit from these classes as I have always stated that they also need to be motivated to find work.

Below is a list of just some of the variations of people I have helped to either gain employment or gain enough confidence and self-belief to feel positive that they will eventually gain employment:

- 18 – 24 year olds just out of college or university
- Those trying to better their promotion prospects
- At risk of redundancy
- Long term unemployed
- Newly redundant
- Young single mums and dads
- Nearly retired male and females
- No work history or experience
- Men/Women who are trying to get back into employment after raising a family for a number of years
- Individuals wanting to change career direction
- Dyslexics
- Ex-offenders
- Managers/team leaders
- Unfair dismissals

I have just mentioned the word *'confidence'*; this is a major *'soft skill'* which is missing from many people. Sadly this could have been routed within an individual from an early age, but I can help you gain this confidence and continue to build upon it.

Low confidence and self esteem certainly plays a negative part within most interviews; this is because an interviewer can see this the minute you walk into the room. I will give you the tools to prevent this from happening again. You will then begin to think more positively about the interview and will be fully equipped to answer any interview question.

So let's begin. I will take you through each session carefully explaining the 'whys' and the 'reasons' behind why each section is an important part of the process and how it links to employability skills.

Enjoy.

STEP 1

IDENTIFY YOUR TRANSFERRABLE SKILLS AND WORK ETHICS

AIM:	To recognise what transferrable skills are and understand the importance of your own work ethics.
OBJECTIVES:	By the end of this session you will be able to:

By the end of this session you will be able to:

- ✓ Demonstrate your knowledge of your own transferrable skills.

- ✓ List at least 5 skills which you can transfer to another job role.

- ✓ Recognise the skills which need to be inserted onto your own C.V.

- ✓ Display awareness of employer's 'Top Ten' wish list.

- ✓ State at least of your 4 work ethics.

What are Transferrable Skills?

In a nutshell:

'Transferrable skills are skills we have gained, learned and acquired over a period of time. These skills can then be transferred to other areas.'

Before I can help you develop your C.V, you must first recognise what skills you have and what skills you didn't realise you have.

I have created an exercise for you to complete, usually my learners would write down their thoughts on the exercise sheet, but for this exercise you can write it down within the book, after all it's yours. But, if you prefer you can always use a spare sheet of paper or use the computer.

These exercises are now going to allow you to think deeper about transferrable skills.

I have just mentioned that you will become aware of the 'Top Ten' employers wish list. This is a list of skills or personality's employers look for in future employers and what they would like their existing employers to have.

Many employers view *personal skills* as being just as important as paper qualifications. Below is a list of personal skills that many employers now regard as an important attribute.

1. Communication
2. Team working
3. Problem solving
4. Confidence
5. Self-esteem and self-belief
6. Time management
7. Flexible and adaptable
8. Planning and organisation
9. Motivation and enthusiasm
10. Self motivated and able to use own initiative

It is important that you recognise these personal skills for being a quality which you have. You will also notice that the above skills contain some of the soft skills I mentioned earlier. This is particularly important if you have limited work experience or no experience at all. You need to focus on these skills; you may need to 'sell' yourself through using these skills.

Put yourself in the position of the employer, would you like to employ someone who had these or even half of these skills? Course you would. These skills can make a company money; they can add value to a company's name. It makes a great place to work, which in turn reduces stress and limits the amount of sickness their workforce takes.

31

Don't under-estimate these skills, claim them. Later on I will help you to 'back up' all of these skills within your interview.

TRANSFERRABLE SKILLS EXERCISE 1

Have a look at the job roles; what skills do you think are needed to carry out the jobs listed? Think hard about these skills, if you have been in one of the mentioned roles, then what are the skills you used? I would suggest you get a blank sheet of paper and really think about the skills needed. You could of course just write it down here; after all it's your book.

Job Role	Skills Needed
Stay at home parent	
Cashier	
Cleaner	
School Dinner Supervisor	
Estate Agent	
Sales Person	
Warehouse Operative	

Transferrable skills needed in each of the job roles.

Job Role	Skills Needed
Stay at home parent	Excellent communication skills, team-work, using own initiative, patience, empathy, punctual, great attendance, excellent time keeper, fantastic sickness record, outstanding organisational skills, budget and money management, Interpersonal skills, problem solving, negotiation, sociability, considerate, common sense, responsible, integrity, flexible, adaptable.
Cashier	Excellent communication skills, team-work, using own initiative, patience, empathy, punctual, great attendance, excellent time keeper, fantastic sickness record, outstanding organisational skills, budget and money management, Interpersonal skills, problem solving, negotiation, sociability, considerate, common sense, responsible, integrity, flexible, adaptable.
Cleaner	Excellent communication skills, team-work, using own initiative, patience, empathy, punctual, great attendance, excellent time keeper, fantastic sickness record, outstanding organisational skills, budget and money management, Interpersonal skills, problem solving, negotiation, sociability, considerate, common sense, responsible, integrity, flexible, adaptable.
School Dinner Supervisor	Excellent communication skills, team-work, using own initiative, patience, empathy, punctual, great attendance, excellent time keeper, fantastic sickness record, outstanding organisational skills, budget and money management, Interpersonal skills, problem solving, negotiation, sociability, considerate, common sense, responsible, integrity, flexible, adaptable.
Sales Person	Excellent communication skills, team-work, using own initiative, patience, empathy, punctual, great attendance, excellent time keeper, fantastic sickness record, outstanding organisational skills, budget and money management, Interpersonal skills, problem solving, negotiation, sociability, considerate, common sense, responsible, integrity, flexible, adaptable.
Warehouse Operative	Excellent communication skills, team-work, using own initiative, patience, empathy, punctual, great attendance, excellent time keeper, fantastic sickness record, outstanding organisational skills, budget and money management, Interpersonal skills, problem solving, negotiation, sociability, considerate, common sense, responsible, integrity, flexible, adaptable.

What skills did you put down?

I have given you examples of these skills and all of them are transferrable.

So do you see where I am going with this? These are everyday skills that you don't realise are great *'Employability Traits'*. Many of you will not have claimed these on your C.V.

Before you may have told me that you're not sure about your skills, if you even have any. Like I said earlier, yes you have got skills you just don't realise this. I hear this time and time again, but unless you have been living in a cave on a remote island with everything at hand for you, then yes you do have skills. Get them down, develop your own awareness of them and claim them.

This is especially important if you have not had much work experience, not gathered many skills to write about on your C.V. I am aware that there are many people who have not had any real work experience at all in their life. Does this mean you have no skill? No, it doesn't. You have many skills employers would love, you just haven't realised it yet.

TRANSFERRABLE SKILLS EXERCISE 2

In the space (or on a separate sheet of paper), have a think about your own skills which you could offer an employer. Don't worry if you can't. Remember, I am going to help you to *develop* your awareness of these skills throughout the employability process.

List your Transferrable Skills here:

1.

2.

3.

4.

5.

6.

7.

I am going to say this again, and I will throughout the book, as I feel it is important to make sure you realise these skills are definitely valuable skills to have. Claim them within your C.V (covered later). Claim them within your interview responses (covered later). You could be lacking in *real work experience* due to other personal issues. You still have experience and that is the key. So if you have limited work experience, think about what you have been doing. Write down any of the previously mentioned skills that you carry out without realising you do it.

You may have even come up with different ones to what I have listed.

WORK ETHICS

What do I mean by work ethics?

These are our ethical thoughts on how we conduct our self at work. These are our thoughts and morals we bring into work. I am not going to go on too much about this. These work ethics are what employers want from future employees' and present employees'.

You have heard me mention 'soft skills', well, these play part of those soft skills. So now it's your turn, what do *you* think your own work ethics are? Have a think about what ethics we should display within the workplace and write down in the space (or on plain paper):

Many people often under-estimate their own work ethics, employers would value the fact that you have *morals* and *principles* about your own work. Below I have listed some of the more common work ethics which employers would value:

- Show up on time
- Excellent sickness/attendance record
- Communicate effectively
- Always willing to '*muck*' in
- Loyal
- Integrity, honest and reliable
- Have a positive work attitude—enhance productivity
- Get along with line managers, co – workers, managers etc
- Work independently
- Dress appropriately
- Take responsibility
- Are able to work with different level of people
- Have accurate self awareness of abilities and skills
- Use problem solving skills
- Willing to go above and beyond for the company
- Flexible attitude
- Dedicated
- Able to use initiative

The skills listed are just a few; work ethics depend on the individual. Let me give you an example of my own work ethics. Within the last 14 years I have had 3 days on the sick. Impressive? So, I would want my prospective employer to know this, so at some point or even within my C.V I would add about my *fantastic* work ethics. As you can see, many of you will have used some of the above keywords within your own C.V. But you will need to prove this and you will do this by backing up your C.V (I will go further into this later). Go on, have another look at the work ethics. Can you think of a time when you have used these ethics? Don't sell yourself short, if you do believe you have fantastic work ethics, sing about it on your C.V.

I am now going to single out; *attendance record*. Do you know why I would do that?

This is because people calling in sick time after time cost companies and employers millions. This is one of the *'bug bears'* with employees. Through experience I will tell you first hand that people abuse the sickness policy. The average amount of holidays the individual has is around 4 weeks. In one place in-particular where I worked for quite a while, there were a few individuals who would save 2 weeks sickness for an extended holiday! They would have their 4 weeks holiday, and always made sure they took 2 weeks sick as they still got paid for it.

If this sounds like you, then sorry. You need to become more work ethical.

Again, this type of behaviour comes down to work ethics or work morals. The choice is yours. But before you take un-necessary sick leave, think of the negative outcomes. A written report on your attendance which could follow you from job to job, maybe it could prevent you getting a job or even promotion.

How do you explain that on your C.V?

Let's have a look at one more from the above list:

- Get along with line managers, co – workers, managers etc

Easier said than done, I know. Again, from my own experience sometimes you may need to bite your tongue when it comes to dealing with line-managers, co-workers etc. And this is coming from a loud mouth Yorkshire lass. Yes, bite your tongue, especially if you are still in your probation period. Now don't get this mixed up with letting people bully you or put on you, no way. What I mean by this is slowly ease yourself into the position, get a feel of the place and the job. Don't go shouting your mouth off on your first day. I always say to people, "*Get your foot in the door and take one step at a time.*"

I remember when I started within Offender Learning, my first few months consisted of me being very quiet, tried my hardest to do the best I could. But there were things I hated about the set up, the '*clique*' which you will find in many work environments, the bitchy comments from men and women. Yes, my first thought would have been to say that I don't particularly like how they have spoken to me or to somebody. But I let it ride; I concentrated on ignoring the looks and comments (I deleted my first words out of respect for you reading this book).

But let me tell you, I certainly let them know (after I had established myself) that they wouldn't mess with me, bully or intimidate me or anyone new to the department. One lady said after I had spoken my mind; "*I can remember when you was so shy, and hardly ever spoke.*" I laughed and replied; "*Well, I waited until my foot was in the door first, and now it is firmly lodged I won't be putting up with this rubbish.*" I loved it. And just for the record, I did speak my mind, obviously in an appropriate manner. This is *assertiveness* (more later on this).

> It is very likely that if you are offered a job, you will be asked to work a 'probation' period.
>
> Usually this is up to 3 months (often longer); within this time span they could *get rid* of you if you don't live up to their expectations. So live by your work ethics to keep your job secure.

RE-CAP AND CONSOLIDATION

So, you should now have a clearer idea of what a transferrable skill is. If you're still unsure re-read about the skills I have listed.

In a nutshell:

> **'Transferrable skills are skills we have gained, learned and acquired over a period of time. These skills can then be transferred to other areas.'**

It doesn't matter if you have not had employment for a while. Look at your everyday actions to get through life. These are transferrable skills. You may have not had much work experience, but think about other experiences which you have used these transferrable skills.

Bringing up a family, what skills do you need? Unpaid carer, what skills did you need?

What are the Top Ten skills employers would like? If you can't remember them go back to the beginning of this session.

What are your own *work ethics*? Ethics basically means what are your own beliefs, morals and values in the work place? Even though there are not pages upon pages on work ethics, don't under-estimate how important these ethics are. Ask people you know if they had to work through a *probation* period. Many will have, I had to work *6 months* within my employability role.

Do you really need time off? Is there really nobody else that can take the dog to the vet? Are you really that ill that you cannot go to work?

If you are having time off within this probation period for no good reason, then you are giving them good reason to finish you. And they are quite within their rights. How will you explain that at your next interview?

What about when it comes to acquiring a reference? Who are you going to use.

BECOME WORK ETHICAL!

Remember

Many employers are not looking for what qualifications you have, many would like to see what **work ethics** and **transferrable skills** you could bring to the company.

Put yourself in an employer's shoes, would you like somebody who had excellent work ethics, or somebody who just looked good on paper because of their qualifications. But did not have good work ethics, transferrable skills or soft skill knowledge?

41

YOUR PERSONAL NOTE PAGE

In the space below, write down any thoughts, ideas and notes you feel will help you throughout the book.

_____

_____

_____

_____

_____

_____

_____

_____

_____

_____

_____

_____

_____

STEP 2

C.V BUILDING

AIM:	Create an outstanding C.V to make you stand out from the crowd. You will be able to list at least 4 strengths and skills.
OBJECTIVES:	

By the end of this session you will be able to:

- ✓ Write down your own Personal Profile.
- ✓ Recognise key words.
- ✓ 'Sing' your praises within your skills and achievements.
- ✓ Tailor your C.V to the required need of the job advert.
- ✓ Write down with confidence what you are good at.
- ✓ Take ownership of your C.V.
- ✓ State the importance of your C.V.

Within this session I will thoroughly explain everything you need to know about your C.V (Curriculum Vitae) and how to make it work for you. When I usually teach this session it could take on average 3 sessions of 3 hours just to do the C.V.

Remember the key here is not to rush, but to look at what you have got to offer the employer. You will never get an interview if an employer does not like what they see on your C.V. So you need to play clever here. You need to get that chance to get to the interview stage. Read every part of this session and you will already be standing out from the crowd. Throughout this session and the book, I will constantly *bang* on about reading the job advertised and the need to alter your C.Vs to fit the job description.

8 WINNING WAYS TO STAND OUT FROM EVERYONE ELSE

Your C.V is your passport into employment. It is your *'glossy brochure'* about yourself. How many C.Vs do you think employers have to search through for each job vacancy? A lot let me tell you.

Your C.V needs to stand out from the crowd. We do this with the following:

1. Keywords
2. Match your C.V to the job advertised (more later)
3. Get all of your main key points on the front page
4. Layout
5. Consistency
6. Research the company and find out their mission statement (covered later)
7. Proof read and don't rely on the spell checker
8. No more than 2 pages

I have broken this section down into small chunks of information, giving examples in depth on what *not* to do and what I *recommend* you should do.

Everyone has a different way of putting their C.V together. I will be using the format in which I have known learners get job interviews with. Again, it may come down to preference, but within this book I will keep to the format which has worked time and time again.

Within this section I will carefully explain each section and why you should or should not place certain information there.

I will then bring it all together with the completed article.

Too many times I have seen the wrong information on a C.V, or too much of irrelevant information. Follow the guidelines and your C.V will soon start advertising you. After all that is what your C.V is. It is an advertisement of you.

8 MUST KNOW QUESTIONS AND ANSWERS ABOUT YOUR C.V

1. How many C.Vs do you have?

The usual reply to this is ONE. Wrong answer. You should always have more than one C.V. You should alter your C.V for every single job you apply for.

This is because each job description or vacancy is different, so you need to tailor your C.V to fit the job description. You do not lie on your C.V; you should be able to back up everything you write on it. Like I said earlier, the key here is to look at what **desirable** and what **essentials** the employers are looking for in their job advert?

2. Do employers read all of your C.V in detail?

No, not usually. They just don't have the time. You will be lucky if they read the first page. So the key here is to capture them within just over half a page (examples given later). This could be all they read, so get them interested in you straight away.

If you have not got their attention, your C.V is in the bin. Harsh, but true. Aim to grab their attention with just over half a page.

3. On average, how long does a prospective employer take to look at your C.V?

Usually within 45 seconds an employer will take to look at your C.V. They may not read it all; just scan it for **key words** to see if you fit the job description. They will just be looking to see if you're of any interest to them and the company.

Again, look at this from an employer's point of view. They may be short staffed, who is going to filter out the 100's or maybe 1000's of C.Vs that land on their desk?

Who has time to read word for word each and every single sentence on a C.V? Let me assure you that nobody has that amount of time, especially if there are a lot of applicants. Time equals to money, time spent looking through C.Vs could be time spent earning the company money.

Have you put your C.V on an internet C.V library? Check your C.V, again, some of the recruiters use computers to filter through C.Vs, if you don't have the correct keywords then the computer is not going to select your C.V.

This is known as the *'faceless filter'*.

One fantastic way to beat the computer generated filter later.

4. Should your qualifications go first?

Not always. This is often a big mistake, especially if it was a long time since you were at school. Employers don't need to know what you did or didn't do 20 years ago in C.S.E's or G.C.S.E's. This is irrelevant; they want to know what you have been doing more recently.

I see each day a variety of C.V's some good and some not so good. One example is of one learner who is in his late 50's. The first thing I saw on his C.V was his qualification, not good ones at that. I said to him, *"Look at your C.V through the eyes of an employer, what are you advertising about yourself?"* *"What information is the employer getting about you?"*

Of course, those who have just finished college or university may want to put their qualifications at the beginning; they may not have any work history or experience. In this situation then I would recommend you put your grades on the first page (unless really bad or you quit halfway through).

But what if you failed your exams? What if you achieved low grades? This will be the first thing on your C.V. Do you want to advertise this to your could-be-employer? Then focus on your work ethics and the soft skills we have just learnt about.

I will give you examples later on; you make up your own mind.

5. How long should it take to do a C.V?

When I ask this question I am always surprised with the answers. The time scale ranges from 1 hour to 2 weeks, the most popular answer is always between 1 and 2 hours. To this I always say that that is not long enough. Your C.V should take at least 5 to 9 hours (depending on experience and employment).

6. How often should you update your C.V?

I would recommend you update your C.V each time you change jobs/roles, gain qualifications and gained any recognition within the workplace; employee of the month, customers service award etc.

7. How to tailor your C.V?

Look at the job or promotion you want to apply for, look at the advertisement. Then, the key here is to take some of their words in what they are looking for and edit your C.V to fit the job description. Research the company and find out what their mission is, what their aims and goals are. Use some of their aims if you can to make them your strengths (only if you can back it up though).

8. Do you lie on your C.V?

Absolutely not. For every piece of information on it, you should be able to *back it up*. You should be able to explain why you are an excellent communicator or team player etc (more later).

On the next few pages we will look at some examples of C.V's.

THE LAYOUT OF YOUR C.V

Generally your C.V should be laid out in the following format or something very similar. It should not contain a border or fancy pictures just to make it pretty. It needs to be straight to the point and you should use plain white paper.

I will go further into examples so don't worry if you're feeling lost, you will get it I promise. I am going to break each of the sections down into smaller chunks.

CONTACT DETAILS

Place your contact details here.

PERSONAL PROFILE

A personal statement about yourself, what have you got to offer, what are you about?

KEY SKILLS AND ACHIEVEMENTS

What have you achieved? What are your key skills? What could you bring to the employer and the company?

CAREER HISTORY

Your history of previous employment, using the most recent first, and then working backwards. You should have a continuous timeline. Make sure the employer can see that you have been *actively seeking work* if you have been unemployed.

EDUCATION AND QUALIFICATIONS

What have you gained qualifications in?

INTERESTS AND HOBBIES

What are your interests and hobbies?

REFERENCES

A brief sentence that they are available upon request.

So that is the headings in which you should have on your C.V. For some people I do understand that you don't have many key skills and achievements (often called key strengths too), so you will need to look at the transferrable skills and work ethic section. Think about which ones fit you and put them in this section.

YOU ARE YOUR C.V – BECOME YOUR C.V

As I mentioned earlier, I don't recommend this book if all you want to do is copy out a C.V. Within the next few pages you will learn how to create your own C.V and edit it when new skills and employment come into place. The biggest thing I want you to get out of this section is that the C.V is yours. The information needs to come from within you. Not somebody down the street who is okay at doing C.Vs, but every piece of information needs to come from inside of you.

COMMON C.V MISTAKES

This is where I am going to break it down further. Here you will see common mistakes that appear on the many C.Vs I have looked at.

CONTACT DETAILS

This may be obvious, but I have seen many people get their own address wrong. How bad does that look? Look at the two examples given, you may think I am being picky, but let me tell you I go through all C.V's with a fine tooth comb to make sure it is the best it can be.

Which do you think is the best address? One or two?

50

ADDRESS 1	ADDRESS 2
Mrs Francis 29 The Crescent Field Leeds West Yorkshire LS26 4GH Tel: 01010101010101 Mobile: 07556985236 Email: tm@hotmail.com	Mrs franis 29 The cresent Field Leeds West yorkshire Ls264gh 01010101010101 07556985236 tm@hotmail.com

Hopefully you have chosen address 1. How many mistakes did you find? These mistakes could be a yes or a no for a job interview. This is could be your first impression.

ADDRESS 1	
✓	**X**
Mrs Francis 29 The Crescent Field Leeds West Yorkshire LS26 4GH Tel: 01010101010101 Mobile: 07556985236 Email: tm@hotmail.com	Mrs franis 29 The cresent Field Leeds West yorkshire Ls264gh 01010101010101 07556985236 tm@hotmail.com

On the next page, I have broken it down further into these mistakes. At this point you may be thinking that people would not make these mistakes. I have yet to see one C.V that has no mistakes on it.

51

Remember, I am stopping you from making mistakes that happen time and time again. People then wonder and question why they are not getting anywhere with their C.V.

Address 2 is wrong.

These are common mistakes I see over and over again.

1. The individual has not put a capital letter for their surname and they have missed the 'c' out of their surname too.
2. Spacing in inconsistent. By that I mean that there is an empty space just before the number 29.
3. The 'c' in Crescent is missing. And, Crescent has not started with a capital letter.
4. Missing capital 'Y' for Yorkshire.
5. The postcode should be all capital letters and a space between (LS26 4GH – this is a very common mistake).
6. Which is the mobile number? Which is the e-mail? Which is the home number?

You may think I have just exaggerated the above example.
Not at all, these mistakes I see each week.

Mrs franis
29 The cresent Field
Leeds
West yorkshire
Ls264gh

01010101010101
07556985236
tm@hotmail.com

As you move on in the book, you will notice that most of the important stuff is on the first page (explained later). But, what a lot of people do to use up space is use half a page (okay, I'm exaggerating) just to put their address on. Stop it now. Use the space wisely.

If you really do want to fit more things on the first page, I could think of much better stuff to put on. Can you? Your transferrable skills we mentioned earlier. So don't go overboard with a massive space filled with your address.

Often learners just shrug their shoulders and say, *"Well the main thing is my qualifications/achievements."* Yes, I agree the qualifications/achievements are important, but, again look at it from an employer's point of view. What does this say about the individual? Doesn't care, not work conscious, untidy, too laid back, no attention to detail, no work ethics, sloppy in work and not professional.

Strong words, but true. I always say to the learners, how would you feel if you had the same qualifications and experience as somebody else, but the employer chose the other person because of the above mistakes.

Exactly, you would be gutted.

EMAIL ALERT, EMAIL ALERT

Look at your email, is it appropriate? If it says something that's personal to you (hot lips, sweet cheeks, smugger etc) then get rid. Yes, your email could put a potential employer off. You could always set up another, more appropriate account which you only use for job applications etc.

SHOULD YOU PUT YOUR AGE ON YOUR C.V?

Now, one last question before I move onto the next section of your C.V. Should you put your date of birth on the contact details?

Again, personal preference but I would say no. Why?

Yes I know about ageism and that it is against the law to be ageist (I have done my level 2 in Equality and Diversity you know). But why should you put your age there, I don't care that the law says you cannot be ageist – people still will look at your age and judge. Again, look at it from an employer's point of view – they want a fit person to load and unload wagons. If you put your age at, let's say 60; what is the first thing that you would think of?

Exactly. Are they fit enough to do the work? Of course they are, but you don't know what is going through their mind. You are being judged and filtered (I will go more into filtering later).

What about a young 20 year old; the job description says *"looking for an experienced mature individual."*

Again, put yourself in the employers' seat. Many are more likely to think that at the age of 20 the individual doesn't have much experience. Wrong, I know; I was a manager at 20! You are being judged.

So, instead of interviewing the individual they are more likely to disregard the C.V through their own judgements.

So let's not leave anything to chance, don't advertise your age (even if your proud of being 28, uhmm I mean 40 like me).

54

KNOCK 'EM' DEAD WITH YOUR PERSONAL PROFILE

PERSONAL PROFILE

The next few lines are very important, and probably one of the hardest things to write on your C.V. Within about 6 – 8 lines you are to give a brief description about *you* and what *you* are about.

Why is this one of the hardest parts of the C.V to write? You are going to '*brag*' about yourself, you are going to '*sell*' yourself. Yes, you are going to 'sing' your own praises.

For a lot of people this does not come naturally, we are not used to doing this. But, believe me, if an employer reads something on your C.V this will probably be part of what they read. This is because within these few lines, an employer will want to see what you are about. They will want a 'glimpse' of what you can do.

When creating your own Personal Profile, take into account the following:

- Don't use words you don't understand
- Do look at the job description
- Do 'sell' your qualities
- Don't put in your hobbies/interests at this stage
- Don't make things up just to impress the employer
- Do make sure you dig deep and advertise your skills
- Do make sure you can '*back up*' what you have written (more later)
- Make it stand out from everyone else, tailor it to the job you are applying for

Look at the examples and see which you think is the best.

Example 1

I am a highly motivated and experienced individual with excellent organisation and communicational skills. I use my own initiative to implement changes to comply with ever changing standards and goals. I have an outstanding ability to motivate and educate a wide range of learners, enhancing their own self belief and confidence. A natural passion to help others to achieve their goals, become self motivated and break down barriers to learning.

Example 2

I am a motivated individual with good organisation skills and I communicate at all levels. Use my own initiative to reach goals. I am able to motivate a range of learners. I am capable of helping others and work well in a team. I enjoy a range of activities and I have a great sense of humour.

So which was the best?

Hopefully you chose example 1. This is what I have used on my own C.V. Believe it or not, it took me ages to come up with it, look at what key words I used. These keywords are vital to finding work in the *Education Sector*.

Let's look more closely at example 1:

> Both of the examples have been used on C.Vs to apply for vacancies within the Education Sector

The secret here are the *key words*, these key words are what you need to think closely about. Look at the words underlined.

These are the key words an employer will scan through and see; these are words used within the education sector. So if you have used these key words, the employer looking at your C.V (*if applying for the Education Sector*) will be captured and will want to read more about you. Different areas of employment will require different key words.

Example 1

I am a <u>highly motivated</u> and experienced individual with <u>excellent organisation</u> and <u>communicational skills</u>. I use my <u>own initiative</u> to <u>implement changes</u> to <u>comply</u> with ever changing <u>standards and goals</u>. I have an <u>outstanding ability</u> to <u>motivate</u> and <u>educate</u> a wide range of learners, <u>enhancing</u> their own <u>self belief</u> and <u>confidence</u>. A <u>natural passion</u> to help others to achieve their goals, become <u>self motivated</u> and <u>break down barriers</u> to <u>learning</u>.

So take a look at example 2:

Example 2

I am a <u>motivated</u> individual with good <u>organisation</u> skills and I <u>communicate</u> at all levels. Use my <u>own initiative</u> to reach goals. I am able to motivate a range of learners. I am capable of helping others and work well in a <u>team</u>. I enjoy a range of activities and I have a great sense of humour.

Okay, not too bad. A few key words have been underlined; that's right a few. That's not good enough though. Remember, we are making you stand out from everybody else. The words in example 2 are a typical variety of words commonly seen on a Personal Profile, and employers are aware of this. In fact, some are *bored* of seeing this.

Your Personal Profile is exactly that. Personal to you. So think about what you have to offer, let me give you another example of the importance of knowing what your Personal Profile is all about.

One young man came onto a course and I knew from his facial expressions (more later) that he hated being there. He had been forced to attend yet another course in order to claim JSA (job seekers allowance – dole money for the older reader). I just said that it is fine; if he is happy with his C.V then I don't believe in re-doing something 'just for the sake of it'. That's one of the problems you see, people are sent from course to course to get their C.V updated. I wouldn't want to go from course to course either. This young man brought his C.V in to show me how good it was and to show me how much he didn't need any help. Yes, you can gather I was starting to feel smug!

Here is the Personal Profile:

I am honest and reliable and I can work well in a team as well as working on my own using my own initiative. I can communicate well and I am looking for work within the Hospitality Industry. I am a good time keeper and I am willing to learn new skills. I enjoy getting jobs done to high standard and I always meet targets set.

Not bad, in fact I liked it. I asked the young man how many places he had sent his C.V off to and he said *"loads."* I asked him in particular which companies he had targeted. His reply was, *"all of the warehouses on the industrial estate."* I was 'gob smacked'. I asked him why he had targeted 'warehouse work', when he clearly stated in his *own* Personal Profile that he was looking for work within the Hospitality Industry.

His reply was; *"I don't understand what Hospitality is, somebody (from another training provider) had told me that it 'sounded good'. I just went along with them."* He had been placed on yet another funded course and he had followed their advice, yes, I agree we all make mistakes with advice from time to time. But to me this was a big mistake. I explained to him what Hospitality was, I then sat with him and asked him about his experience and which area he would like to gain work in. With this I spent more time with him and I gave him advice on what I would use. He thanked me for my time and said that he had learnt more in 30 minutes than he had on a 4 week training course.

"Your Personal Profile is about you; make sure you know everything on it!
Don't blame others for a rubbish C.V it's your responsibility."

PERSONAL PROFILE SENTENCES

To help you get used to writing your own Personal Profile, I have come up with a few ideas. But, please remember, this is about *you*. You need to make sure you stand out from the crowd, but *do not lie*. You will need to give examples of everything on your C.V (further on in the book). I am just writing down good examples, not the whole profile, that way **you** are creating it yourself (with a little help). Many of these profiles can be used within other areas too.

RETAIL PROFILE

The main focus within retail is the customer and reaching targets. How you communicate and go that extra mile for both the customer and the company. Think about what an employer would want to see.

- ✓ Strong sense of excellent customer skills
- ✓ Understand the importance of going the extra mile for the customer and for the company
- ✓ Excellent interpersonal skills and possess an outstanding ability to communicate at all levels
- ✓ With a methodical approach to planning and organising
- ✓ Work well with others and I have the ability to motivate and lead by example
- ✓ Tolerant and understanding nature towards others
- ✓ Energetic with a positive outlook
- ✓ Uses own initiative to develop solutions to maximise sales

- ✓ Pro-active with a keen eye for detail
- ✓ Self driven and able to set and meet targets

Try putting that together:

> I have excellent communication skills which I use at a variety of levels to ensure both the company and the customer is always satisfied. I am always willing to go out of my way to ensure maximum sales and maximum customer service is given at all times. I enjoy working as part as a team and I have the ability and initiative to work alone.

Or

> I have an outstanding level of customer service skills which I have used to gain excellent results and to meet targets. I use my passion for success to keep me self motivated and flexible to meet the changing needs of the customer and company. I have a calm nature and I am a natural with dealing with members of the public.

Look at the key words; this is where you would manipulate your C.V to fit the job description. Get used to looking at what the company is looking for. Make sure though, that you can fully back up everything on your C.V (more later).

60

WAREHOUSE PROFILE

So what do you think the main focus in this area would be? Certainly the ability to be able to work in a team. You should also have a keen eye for detail and focus on the fact that you are capable of working to deadlines and targets.

- ✓ Reliable and dependable in meeting targets
- ✓ Excellent communicator
- ✓ Team player
- ✓ Adaptable and flexible
- ✓ Solid approach to achieving tasks
- ✓ Well organised; great time keeper and planner
- ✓ Active and dynamic approach to work and getting things done
- ✓ Systematic and logical
- ✓ Able to multi-task and prioritise work
- ✓ Accurate
- ✓ Self aware
- ✓ Self driven, able to set goals and lead by example

An example of a Personal Profile here would be:

I am an active and dynamic individual who can be relied upon to meet set targets and goals. Been adaptable and flexible within my previous roles to ensure a high standard of work has been carried out at all times. A well organised individual who can productively work in a systematic and logical manner, playing part of a team to get the best of myself and others. Communicates effectively and efficiently when speaking with others.

61

Or

A determined and dependable person with excellent people skills. I work well with others and I am able to motivate and encourage my team workers. I have a keen eye for detail and I feel I am precise and thorough throughout my roles/tasks. An excellent communicator with an enthusiastic and energetic approach to all tasks. Able to meet and exceed targets and strive to carry out tasks to the highest standard.

If you're unsure what qualities you need to work within this environment then Google:

What qualities do I need to work in a warehouse? It's as simple as that.

BUSINESS ADMINISTRATION PROFILE

What skills do you think you would need to advertise in your Personal Profile within this area? Certainly you would need to be able to multi-task and be organised? What about using your initiative and integrity? So get it down.

- ✓ Uses own initiative to develop effective solutions
- ✓ Methodical approach to planning and organising
- ✓ Ability to communicate at all levels
- ✓ Identifies and develops opportunities
- ✓ Self aware – always willing to learn and grow
- ✓ An efficient time manager
- ✓ Able to communicate messages, written and oral accurately
- ✓ Excellent interpersonal skills
- ✓ Conscientious and uses integrity

✓ Great team player – adaptable and flexible

✓ Able to implement new filing structures to benefit efficiency

Example of Business Admin Personal Profile:

I have an adaptable and flexible approach to any job I do, using my calm and dependable nature to meet deadlines and targets. I have the ability to plan and organise my time to ensure tasks are prioritised to meet the demands of the company. Using my integrity to comply with Data Protection and customer loyalty I am fully aware of protocol and procedures. I have a methodical approach to work but uses own initiative to seek alternatives.

Or

I have sensitive and patient interpersonal skills with a superb ability to communicate effectively either face to face or through the phone. I have an energetic and positive outlook which often inspires others. I have a proven record of being immaculate and precise when dealing with paperwork and can use the in-out tray approach to prioritise my work. I have a caring and compassionate nature which has made working as part of a team more enjoyable.

As always, the trick here is to see what qualities you need to carry admin duties to a high standard. If you're not sure, then 'Google' it.

63

CHILDCARE PROFILE

In your Personal Profile, what characteristics and key words do you think would be appropriate here? What is the most important thing an employer would want from a prospective employee? The ability to work with children!

So what lines or words would you put on your Personal Profile if you were applying for a position of childcare?

- ✓ Energetic
- ✓ Communicate with children and parents
- ✓ Innovative (able to use own imagination)
- ✓ Stimulating
- ✓ Fun-loving
- ✓ Enthusiastic
- ✓ A natural ability to support children grow and develop
- ✓ Motivated
- ✓ Caring nature
- ✓ Uses empathy to deal with problems
- ✓ Creative
- ✓ Adaptable to individual needs
- ✓ Team working skills
- ✓ Able to solve problems quickly

So a Personal Profile here would be similar to the examples given:

I have a natural ability to bring out the best in children, using my fun and enthusiastic approach to promoting well being. I have the ability to create activities which will help the children develop and become confident in their growth. Working in a team to create innovative ways in helping the children use their own imagination and become confident in their abilities.

Or

I am an enthusiastic and energetic person who has a natural ability to bring out the best in the children. Using my fantastic people skills I quickly build up a rapport with both children and their parents. Using my adaptable and flexible approach, I am always working to meet the needs of the individuals and recognise different ways in which I can help create imaginative and stimulating activities.

Again, if you're unsure about the qualities, then research or ask somebody who has a child about their own qualities and what they feel constitutes a fantastic childcare assistant.

65

CLEANING INDUSTRY PROFILE

Don't under-estimate the job title of 'cleaner', this all important job role will certainly need a fantastic Personal Profile. What abilities do you think you will need?

Example phrases:

- ✓ Excellent communication skills
- ✓ Can do attitude
- ✓ Physically fit and able to perform demanding duties
- ✓ Conscientious at all times
- ✓ High standard of work
- ✓ Flexible and adaptable approach
- ✓ Dedicated and competent
- ✓ Passion about hygiene
- ✓ Understands and adheres to all COSHH regulations

Take a look at possible profiles you could use.

So a typical Personal Profile here would be:

An enthusiastic and competent cleaner with a great deal of experience of working within both commercial and residential buildings. Able to work part of at team and a responsible nature with excellent people skills. Passionate about making a pleasant environment for both customers and staff and all work carried out to a high standard.

66

Or

> A dedicated and competent person who possesses excellent communication skills and a passion for ensuring environments are kept clean and tidy to a very high standard. Easily meets the demands of the customers and staff and is self motivated and physically fit. I always ensure that all COSHH regulations are adhered to and understand the need to report defective equipment.

No matter what type of job you are going for, you will be competing against other people. I have known one learner go for a cleaning job and was grilled within the interview as though she was going for a managerial role. For every job, sell yourself and your skills.

SECURITY PROFILE

Again, look at what typical Personal Profile would be best suited here:

- ✓ Resourceful and flexible
- ✓ Promoting a safe environment
- ✓ Respond effectively to any emergency or situation
- ✓ Possessing excellent written and oral communication skills
- ✓ Ability to handle conflict tactfully
- ✓ Able to respond quickly
- ✓ Outstanding communication skills to ensure safety
- ✓ Can work within a team but equally can use own initiative
- ✓ Dealing with hostile customers
- ✓ Reporting of incidents quickly

67

✓ Multi-task to ensure all areas covered

✓ Experience of night patrol and securing building perimeters

✓ Reporting incidents quickly and effectively

✓ Monitor and authorisation

So a typical Personal Profile here would be:

A resourceful and flexible individual who uses own initiative to promote a safe environment with fantastic written and oral communication skills. I have the ability to respond to situations in a timely manner and have extensive experience of handling conflict tactfully. Experience of managing large events and staff to work alongside other organisations.

Or

I am an experienced and enthusiastic security guard looking or a position within an exciting and ambitious company. I am self motivated and possess fantastic communication skills. Understanding the demand of the company and dealing with conflict in a respectful and courteous manner. Able to multi-task and adapt to the company and the customers' needs whilst maintaining professionalism at all times.

As with all of the above profiles, make sure you adapt it so that it includes keywords of the job advertised.

68

GET INTO THE HABIT

All the way through the process of searching, applying and in the actual interview you need to get into one habit. *Researching* the company and finding out your own keywords. I will keep on mentioning this because you really do need to go more in depth within this process.

What keywords are they looking for? What could make you stand out from everyone else? Your knowledge, that's what.

IT'S ALL ABOUT YOU

So you're beginning to understand the importance of Personal Profiles. Again, it could be the only thing the employer or interviewer looks at. Stand out from the crowd. Make sure you like your Personal Profile. Don't be shy about saying how excellent, fantastic or superb you are; believe me, other people going for the same job won't be. This comes down to being confident about *you*; I know it's a hard thing for most of us, but it is a major fact when applying for jobs is having the *confidence*. I don't need to remind you of the current un-employment figures, but there are jobs out there, be confident within your Personal Profile.

The Personal Profiles given do not just need to be within the area I have put them under. You can use any of the sentences which you feel comfortable with. I say comfortable, this is because many people have told me that their Personal Profile has been created for them, they have not had any say in it therefore they don't like what has been put. Before you move on to the next stage I just need to remind you about your Personal Profile.

69

It is about you. Make sure you can *back up* everything that is on your C.V. Make sure you have read it word for word. Honestly, I cannot tell you how many times I have looked at a learners' Personal Profile and found large words, spelling mistakes and things that are just not true. Think how foolish you would feel if you were sat in front on an interviewer and the following happened:

Interviewer: "Okay, I can see from your C.V that you have a pragmatic approach; can you give me an example of this?"

If you wrote the word 'pragmatic' yourself then fine, but in this example the learner had not really had much input into *his* C.V. He was caught out.

The above example actually happened when I did a one to one interview. He, and others like him don't realise the importance of the Personal Profile.

Don't get caught out, make sure you are your C.V.
Don't rely on somebody else (even professionals) creating
you a fantastic C.V
You're responsible for it nobody else!

YOUR SKILLS AND ACHIEVEMENTS

KEY SKILLS AND ACHIEVEMENTS

Within this area you need to bullet point your key skill and achievements. I say to the learners that you can split this section into two parts; key skills and then another section for achievements. Again, this depends on your work experience. Generally for those that may not have many key skills or achievements you can put them together.

70

The key here is, like mentioned earlier is to *'spoon feed'* the employer your skills. By this I mean make it easy for them to read and pick out your key words which you have added.

If the job description stated that they needed a flexible and adaptable individual, then one of your key skills is that; *'you are an adaptable and flexible individual'*, I will bring it all together later on so don't worry about this. As you can see from the example below, this section has been put into two.

It surprises me that so many people forget their 'soft skills' and 'work ethics', these are skills remember. Think long and hard about your experiences, have you motivated others? Have you gone above and beyond? Claim it. Write it down. This example is my own, this is tailored for the educational sector, I have split mine as I have quite a lot to put down (better than when I first left school).

I stated at the beginning that you would not find loads of C.Vs to simply copy, this is because you first need to be aware of all those skills you have. Then you can *own* your C.V and understand everything that's on it. Too many people are quick to blame others for their own C.V. Take responsibility and do it yourself.

I cannot stress enough how important it is for you to come up with the right keywords and sentences in your C.V. Remember I teach from experience and past mistakes, so trust me you need to spend time doing your C.V. Never put anything down that you cannot *justify* or give examples for. I assure you, if you look inside yourself enough, you will be able to find these examples I promise.

If you need to, then go back to the previous session on *transferrable skills*. Do you need to add some of these to your key strengths/ achievements?

On the next few pages I will be demonstrating how to set out your *key strengths* and/or *achievements*. This can vary due to the different amount of experience a person has.

71

The following has been taken from my own C.V:

Key Achievements:

- **Nominated** for, and won '**Employee of the Month**' in November 2011, this recognised my **passion** and **determination** to **support** my learners in gaining employability skills.
- **Implemented, created** and **delivered** a P.E.T course for ThomsonTUI for overseas childcare reps.
- **Adapted** and **changed** the ICT course and **implemented** the necessary changes to **push forward** the course to become **successful**.
- **Achieved 100% success rate** as of 2009-2011.
- **High retention figures** on all courses delivered.
- **Examiner and assessor**, liaising with OCR with **0 errors** recorded on all exams submitted.
- **Gained a grade 1** (outstanding) in my last three teaching observations.
- Worked with Functional Skills co-ordinator to **successfully implement** and teach on the new Functional Skills ICT course, with a **100% pass rate**.
- **Recreated** and **ran** the Alcohol Awareness course ensuring all **barriers to learning** where met **efficiently** and all information was current to meet set standards and criteria.
- **Recreated** Healthy Living course on Social and Life Skills, again ensuring all learner needs were met. Setting out the course to fit in with set standards and criteria ensuring portfolios would demonstrate competency of the learner.
- **Successful manageress** of a retail shop for 10 years. The day-to-day running of a retail shop, including staffing, wage costs and budgeting, stocktaking, **promoting goods** and **customer care**.

72

Quite lengthy I know, but I need to get these qualities down on the first page, I want an employer to be *eager* about reading more about me. I want to stand out from everybody else. I must mention that I have only added bold to text to make it stand out. Please don't do this on your C.V.

Sadly though, we cannot foresee exactly what an employer is looking for. Research the company and see if you can adapt their aims, values, goals, visions and mission statement to your own skills.

WHAT ABOUT YOUR KEY SKILLS?

I have put an example of my own achievements, yes I could have put it with my qualifications but for my own preference I have kept it here. Again, it is only in bold to highlight the key skill, don't you do this on your C.V.

- **A1 assessor**.
- Gained **QTLS** through continual **professional development**.
- **Excellent knowledge** of Microsoft Word, Excel, PowerPoint, Publisher and Database
- Maintain **professional standards** and keep knowledge **current** through IFL **Professional Development (Equality and Diversity** Level 2, Financial Capabilities Level 3)
- **Excellent disposition** to offer and **promote soft skills** and **motivation** to **diverse** learners
- **Diverse teaching methods** to **enhance learning** and to **promote equality** and **diversity**
- **Excellent sickness record**. 0 days absent within the last 5 years and 3 days absent within the last 14 years

A Great Trick To Stand Out from The Crowd

Here, again I have added key words in which future employers will recognise, therefore, *spoon feeding*; making it easier for them to read without getting bored. Remember; don't highlight these words on your C.V.

This way, again I am trying to capture the attention of my potential employer. Looking at a job description I would see what the company is looking for and if I feel that I have *some* of the skills I will add them here (or Personal Profile). Manipulating my C.V so that it meets the needs of the prospective employer is one sure fire way to get noticed. You won't get an interview if they don't like you on paper.

So look at the job description, see which parts you can pinch and then copy them into your C.V. I cannot get this point across enough; you need to be able to give examples of everything you have on your C.V. Just in case the interviewer really grills you about the information on your C.V. After all, this is the only *snap shot* they have of you.

Just imagine that the employer is only going to look at just over half a page of your C.V. Try doing this; print off your C.V and then cover up half of it with a blank piece of paper. Now ask yourself, *"What information is the employer getting here about what I can offer the company?"*

Be honest, and if the answer is, *"Not a lot."* Then change it. Try and use the same template layout as I have used. Then do the same. Keep asking yourself questions as if you were the employer. This is getting you used to being self aware.

What About Your Own Key Skills?

Look at what you have achieved. No matter how small you may think it is, again another hard task to do. Why? Why is it so hard to write down our skills? This is because we do these things each day so we don't recognise it as a skill. We take for granted (and so do some employers) these skills and don't recognise them for an important skill which they are.

74

Let me write down a few examples of skills, again, make sure you can back up your skills with an example (in case they question you at an interview about it, more on that later).

When I teach people about *Key Skills* and *Achievements* I often get blank looks. They usually say, *"Tracey, I don't have any skills and I can't think of any achievements."* Think back a few pages; think about the *soft skills* and *work ethics*.

Some of the learners have a lifetime of experience, especially the older ones. You may need to go down *'memory lane'* here, because you have skills and achievements, you just don't see it yet. Another lady informed me that she has been a *"stay at home mum";* therefore she cannot have any skills or achievements. WRONG. When I get this reply, I usually ask the person a number of questions on: time keeping, cooking, cleaning, and responsibility, multi-tasking, motivation and communication etc. Can you see where I am going with this?

One lady in particular said the above to me, I chatted with her about her work life and experience. She then said, *"Well, I did win outstanding customer service award – twice."* I looked at her in bewilderment. I said to her, *"Where is that on your C.V?"* Again, because it was something she did without realising she did not recognise this as a skill.

So think about your career experience, think about your employers' words, and think about any recognition within your life. These are the skills and achievements.

The trick here is to look deeper into what you have done. Have you been awarded *'Student of the year'*? Have you been awarded or nominated for your services? Have you been recognised for excellent time keeping and attendance? Have you ever led a team? What about been a natural motivator? Do you motivate and how do you inspire others? I know I have, it's taken me a long time to realise this though.

No matter how small or unimportant you may think it is, get it down.

75

Think about your transferrable skills and work ethics which I covered in session1.

TAKE OWNERSHIP OF WHAT YOU HAVE DONE

Take ownership now, own what you have done. If you're unsure, ask your partner, children, friends or anyone. At this point I would normally have a group discussion and find answers from the group. It is very surprising how we can find the answers from outside ourselves.

On the next page I have given you a list of key skills; these have been taken from all areas of employment.

Do any of them resemble your skills? Do any of them sound something similar to what you have done? Okay, so you may change the wording, but the ideas are there.

A LIST OF POSSIBLE KEY SKILLS:

This list could go on and on so I am just giving you a helping hand to start you off. It may just make you realise and jog your memory to your own situation:

- ✓ Strong motivational skills.
- ✓ Excellent team player and values opinion of others.
- ✓ Able to prioritise tasks to ensure company targets are met.
- ✓ Can demonstrate effective sales presentations on a face to face level.
- ✓ Have a competitive attitude and can thrive under pressure.
- ✓ Passionate and dedicated to previous company, building moral where necessary.
- ✓ A genuine passion to provide quality service to the public, thereby, maintaining a positive company image.
- ✓ Excellent motivation and enthusiasm for all tasks undertaken.
- ✓ Outstanding ability to be flexible to meet the needs of both employers and customers.
- ✓ Delivered exceptional customer service.
- ✓ Always believe in going that extra mile for the customer.

76

A List Of Possible Key Skills (Continued):

- ✓ Proven ability to lead, build and motivate successful teams.
- ✓ Enthusiasm for creating delicious food and providing excellent service.
- ✓ Good at working under pressure and at a high standard.
- ✓ I am flexible and adaptable, responding to customer and company needs including variable work patterns.
- ✓ I am eager to tackle problems or issues in a way that will satisfy the needs of others.
- ✓ Working within Health & Safety guidelines.
- ✓ Able to cope with pressure.
- ✓ Can summarise key issues.
- ✓ Undertaken all in house training events to keep knowledge current and up to date.
- ✓ Natural ability to lead and motivate a team.
- ✓ Ability to risk assess and carry out reports.
- ✓ Excellent geographical sense.
- ✓ Outstanding organisational skills.
- ✓ Proven influencer and negotiator.
- ✓ Achieving targets in a dynamic and complex business environment.
- ✓ Building and maintaining strong and effective relationships with customers and suppliers.
- ✓ Strong motivational and influential people skills.
- ✓ Experience of managing people and driving business performance.
- ✓ A proven ability to hit and exceed targets.
- ✓ Flexible and able to respond positively to change.
- ✓ Able to plan, prepare, do and review child friendly activities.
- ✓ Successful supervisor within a retail industry.
- ✓ Adaptable to individual needs, caring and able to work using my own initiative.
- ✓ I have excellent communication skills and have the ability to adjust the level of required communication to meet the needs of the company.
- ✓ Desire to achieve.
- ✓ Exceeded targets.

<u>Remember</u>

I cannot put your skills down here; I don't know what you have all done. *You* do though, so think hard about yourself. Don't sell yourself short, don't under-estimate what you have achieved.

Always think to yourself that the person in front or behind you will be claiming much more, be brave, and be confident. Claim these skills. This is where I really need you to 'dig deep' inside yourself. You may need to ask somebody who you trust to help you come up with a list of qualities you may have over looked. As I say and I will always say it, I am speaking from experience, so I do know how hard it is at times to find the qualities inside of you.

LIMITED OR NO EXPERIENCE

This is one of the most common problems I come across, especially within the 18 – 24 year old group. You have all heard the words, *"They want experience, but how do I get the experience?"* Yes it is true that many employers are wanting those who have relevant experience. How do you get through this barrier? You wow them at the interview. So follow the tips in the C.V steps, and when you arrive at your interview you will be so full of self belief and enthusiasm that they will be able to see your full potential. They will look beyond the experience and see that you have a lot to offer the company. We will cover interview skills later.

KEY SKILLS/STRENGTHS AND ACHIEVEMENTS

Within this section, as you can see with my own, I have quite a few achievements to put down. This is where I cannot help you or give you examples. This has got to come from what *you* have achieved, no matter how small you may think it is; you have achieved something.

- Were you part of a team that created something?
- Do you use your outstanding communication skills? Of course you do, communication is a two way process; speaking and listening.

78

- Have you reached your sales target?
- Have you used initiative and done something; (it could be a small matter of moving a display from **A** to **B** to maximise sales)?
- Have you motivated a team?
- Have you come up with ideas; used your own imagination?
- Have you gone that extra mile for somebody, if so what did you do?

So have a look, don't worry if you can't think of anything straight away, you will think of something I promise.

Are you a self – motivated and determined person? Yes you are. You have bought this book therefore that is self motivation and determination to change your employment status. Simple as that, you don't need to go too wordy or deep into things, just get on your C.V what you have done.

ARE YOU LOOKING FOR PROGRESSION OR PROMOTION?

You will see within the *key achievement* section, I have added a small sentence on what I have achieved. This makes me look competent. If you want to go for promotion or progression, then it is vital that you show your competence.

You should only write a couple of sentences at the most. Your employer or interviewer will start getting bored. So get it down in a *short, sharp* sentence and to the point.

As with many jobs, we get used to doing skilled tasks day in day out. So look at what you do in the space of a day, week, month etc and write down as much as you can on a piece of paper. You will be really surprised as what skills you actually use. This may be a good point to get a work colleague on board to help you.

How To Use Your Appraisals

Look at your appraisals, what positives have been mentioned? A lot of people I have worked with over the years would dread the 'appraisal time'. I used to love it. This is me being a bit big headed here, but I knew that it would probably be one of the only times I got some feedback on my work.

So think about yours. Do you need a copy? If so try getting one, your line manager or team leader should be able to help you with this. Read the input, and take all of the positives and claim this on your C.V.

Explaining Your Career History

CAREER HISTORY

Here you need to start with your most recent job. A common mistake is to put your very first job role here. No, look at it from an employer's point of view. Do they need to know where you worked first? No they don't. You need to make it easier for them to see what you have been doing more recently.

Example 1:

Sales Assistant

Shoe shoe Ltd - 12/08/1988 - 18/08/1997

Brief Duties: Working on the tills and handling cash. Stocking shelves, helping customers. (*This is brief just to get the point across*).

It doesn't really matter what you put it was too long ago. They are losing interest now.

Example 2:

Course Tutor

Education and Employability - 01/09/2008 – 12/05/2012

Brief Duties: Fully co-ordinated, implemented and delivered ITQ from E3 to Level 2. Working with unemployed individuals to gain employment skills; Soft skills (communication and confidence), CV's and interview skills.

So you can see what this person is doing *now*. Remember, the people looking at your C.V may have 100's if not 1000's to look through. They don't give a monkey's what you did when you left school, especially if it was such a long time ago.

This is more important if you are over the age of around 27 as you would have around 10 years work experience to put down. So, work your way back through time and you can then create a *timeline* of your employment history. Life experience can also say such a lot about a person.

VOLUNTARY WORKERS

I have seen many C.Vs which miss out a vital part; *voluntary work.* This is especially important if you have not had a paid job for a while, at least the employer knows that you are doing something constructive with your time. Even if you are in employment, if you have done any voluntary work, get it down. It can say a lot about a person.

Think of any charity that you have maybe help to set up. One lady in particular played a huge part in securing a Lottery grant to help set up a charity. Had she claimed this? No, again we don't claim some very important things on our C.V.

81

Your Career Timeline

So, let's see an example of how your *timeline* should look. The example below is again from my own C.V; I have cut it down for eligibility but look at the timeline. You will notice that at one point I had two jobs, both part time. You will also see that I have left off my managerial role and my break in employment. This is because I needed the extra space to focus on what I have been doing now, not fifteen years ago.

Employability Tutor
19/07/2011 – Present - Employability Provider
Working with unemployed individuals to help them gain 'intensive' employment skills; soft skills (communication and confidence), CVs and interview skills. Receiving outstanding feeding back from all clients/learners who have now gained employment or who are in a position to face the interviewer with confidence.

ITQ Course Tutor
01/09/2008 – 18/07/2011 - The Manchester College
Fully co-ordinated, implemented and delivered ITQ from E3 to Level 2; assisted the implementation and creation of Functional ICT.

Sessional I.T Tutor
02/05/2006 – 31/08/2008 - The Manchester College
Created and delivered a wide range of programs ensuring criteria met on first assessment.

Sessional I.T Lecturer
08/10/2005 - 01/05/2006 - Wakefield College
Supported teaching assistants require and recognise ways of delivering and differentiating topics within ICT.

Warehouse Operative
11/04/2000 - 11/04/2006 - Argos Distribution Centre
Using excellent accuracy skills to pick and pack a wide variety of items to a high standard.

82

How To Explain Breaks In Your Career

As you can see from the timeline, you are displaying a continuous line of activity. But what happens if you haven't got a continuous line of activity? Below I have given an example of how this should look:

Cleaner

June 2008 – Present – Cleaners 'R' us.

Working as part of a team and responsible for various cleaning duties to ensure the cleanliness of the building.

July 2007 – June2008 –Actively seeking employment.

Due to the end of a contract I was made redundant, I have been actively looking for employment since.

Toilet Attendant and Cleaner

January 2000 – July 2007 – Mop N Bucket Ltd.

Dealing with the public and ensuring all standards of hygiene were high. Working as part of team to get excellent results.

December 1998 – December 2000 – Actively seeking employment.

Due to major redundancies within the company I was made redundant. Within this time I used my own initiative to gain numerous qualifications which are listed below.

Literacy level 1
Numeracy Level 1
ICT level 1

As you can see in the example, there are a couple of incidents where the individual has been out of work. Rather than leave this out, which many people do, keep the timeline going and briefly give an explanation. You may need to expand on this within an interview.

As you can see, I have given a small amount of information about my career break. Do not give too much information out at this stage, especially if you were sacked or left under a black cloud.

YOU'VE BEEN OUT OF WORK WHILE RAISING A FAMILY

Okay, we have taken a look at what examples you can put down if you don't have a continuous line of employment. But what about if you are returning to work after been a *'stay at home mum/dad'* for several years?

This is how I would recommend you do this: first and most importantly, create an *outstanding 'Personal Profile'*. You need to get the reader captivated. Once you have wrote about 6 – 8 lines about yourself have a look at transferrable skills.

Identify your transferrable skills which I mentioned earlier:

- Excellent communication skills
- Willing to undertake any challenge or role
- Willing to learn new skills
- Outstanding organisational skills
- Excellent ability to perform under pressure
- Adaptable and flexible
- Able to work on own initiative
- Displays empathy, patience and understanding

Have a think of other things you may have done with your time whilst raising your family. Have you volunteered to help out within schools? Did you become an active member of the PA (parents association)? Have you given your time to go on school trips? Have you volunteered your services to an organisation? Think about how you have spent your time.

Whilst out of work believe me you will have gained more skills than you first thought. I'm a parent of two boys and I certainly know that bringing up a family is often harder than working for a company. Yes, and it's a lot less pay too.

Seriously, think about what you have achieved. Remember, you have life experience. Maybe more than you realise. Think positive and this will show (more on this later).

PROMOTION OR PROGRESSION

Okay, you already have a job but you are wanting to climb the employment ladder. Think of your job role, what key skills can, and have you achieved? Look at my first part of the C.V. You can afford to use the extra space to really lay it on thick about what you have done for the company and what you can do for them in the future. At this stage, it really is important that they get what you are about as opposed to what you may have done years ago that just may not be relevant anymore. The key is still the same; *sell yourself*.

85

YOUR EDUCATION AND QUALIFICATIONS (EVEN IF YOU HAVE NONE)

EDUCATION AND QUALIFICATIONS

This is where you will put your most recent qualifications and/education. Put it in order of most recent qualification.

The example I have given below is my own, as you can see I have not put down my education history. Why do you think this is so? Well, let me tell you. I mentioned earlier that I left school with no qualifications, so why advertise the fact that I was a *'tearaway',* who couldn't be bothered with education. (Really hope my children don't read this). I bet this sounds familiar to many of you. School and education was of no importance to me back then, that's why I decided to go back to college in my 30's. My numeracy skills were none existent, but like I say;

"Take ownership, support is there and it is often free, so use it."

So, if like me your recent qualifications make up for the lack of qualifications gained at school, miss your school history out. Just think like an employer, do they really need you to put down how little you did 20 odd years earlier? Should I really put down that the only thing I left school with was a bottle of cider? No definitely not.

Look at the qualifications I have now. Everyone was a struggle to achieve, but like I will keep saying to you:

"If you don't help yourself, don't expect anyone else to help you."

86

EDUCATION AND QUALIFICATIONS

- A1 Assessor – Manchester College - 2011
- QTLS – Through IFL - 05/03/2010
- Certificate in Education (Cert Ed) – Huddersfield University Level 5/6 - 06/06/2008
- Transforming Learning with Information Learning Technology Level 4 Subject Specialism - 28/12/2005
- JEB Diploma in ICT Practice and Principles Level 3 - 02/06/2005
- Learning to Teach Online (Lettol) – Level 3 - 06/02/2006
- Adult Numeracy Level 2 - 10/12/2010
- Adult Literacy Level 2 – 15/03/2009
- ECDL Level 2 - 03/09/2003
- Advanced ECDL Word Level 3 - 27/02/2004
- NVQ Customer Services Level 3 - 09/09/1996

BEWARE: INTERESTS AND HOBBIES COULD DO YOU MORE HARM THAN GOOD

Personal Interests and Hobbies

We're nearly at the end of the C.V now. This part is where you briefly give an overview of what you like to do in your spare time. Be aware though, certain things should not be put down. Look at the list below to see if you can see anything wrong with it:

Personal Interests:

1. Loyal supporter of Leeds United and enjoy watching them within the football season.
2. Enjoys shooting rabbits and birds on a weekend to help me relax.
3. Dedicated aggressive skater
4. Enjoys clubbing each weekend.

87

Okay, so what do you think is wrong with that? These interests are from actual C.Vs. Again, we often under-estimate what the employer could be thinking. Don't leave anything to chance, don't allow yourself to be filtered out of the door with yet another rejection.

The above are common interests I see each week. Now, look from it from another angle. You're the employer and you're an avid Man Utd fan. Would you entertain a rival football fan? I know it's extreme, but like I said earlier, I want you to cover everything that could stop you gaining employment. I am not saying this scenario would, but we are not leaving it to chance.

I certainly know somebody from my own family who would certainly not entertain a rival footie/rugby fan. I know you may be the best worker going, but again, you're leaving yourself wide open to a rejection letter.

The shooting of rabbit's scenario made me laugh when I saw this on a learner's C.V. Yes they are really proud of their shooting expertise, but what I said to them was, "*Your prospective employer is a keen animal rights activist, how do you think they would feel about reading about your hobbies?*" Again, extreme I know but just be aware of what other's may think. You have no idea who is sifting through your C.V. You have no idea their thoughts, values and morals.

The dedicated aggressive skater was a lovely young man, good manners and polite. I explained that from an employer's point of view I would not be impressed with the word 'aggressive'. I explained that he comes across on his C.V that he is moody, got anger problems and he certainly isn't a people person. All very wrong, but the interviewer is not going to waste time in finding out. The C.V will most likely go in the bin. This young man agreed and decided to put down; 'enjoys sports', boring compared, I know. But the aim is to get to the interview stage.

The last scenario regarding clubbing every weekend, may tell an employer that you may take Monday's off due to a *mysterious illness*. Yes, a hangover. Again, reword it. We are not going to let anything stand in the way of getting a job.

88

We don't want them to have a shred of doubt. What if the position you have applied for is to work flexible hours and weekends at short notice. Don't set yourself up for a fail before you've even got your toe in the door.

When I was given the opportunity to run an 'alcohol awareness' course, my first thought was; *"Bloody hell, I always stink of stale ale on a Monday. How can I do that?"* Obviously I didn't tell them about my *'benders'*. So I always try and not put something like *'socialising'* down. They may just think you're a party animal.

You will soon realise that life and work has a wealth of opportunities waiting. Some may be small; other opportunities may be the break you need to show off even more of your skills.

I know these scenarios may seem daft, extreme and judgemental but look at it from an employers' point of view. Would you risk setting somebody on? Don't allow yourself to be filtered out of the exit door.

Just change some of the words slightly.

THE COMPLETED C.V

PERSONAL PROFILE:

I am a highly motivated and experienced individual with excellent organisation and communicational skills. I use my own initiative to implement changes to comply with ever changing standards and goals. I have an outstanding ability to motivate and educate a wide range of learners, enhancing their own self belief and confidence. A natural passion to help others to achieve their goals, become self motivated and break down barriers to learning.

KEY ACHIEVEMENTS

- Nominated for, and won 'Employee of the Month' in November 2011, this recognised my passion and determination to support my learners in gaining employability skills.
- Implemented, created and delivered a P.E.T course for ThomsonTUI for overseas childcare reps.
- Adapted and changed the ICT course and implemented the necessary changes to push forward the course to become successful.
- Achieved 100% success rate as of 2009-2011.
- Gained a grade 1 (outstanding) in my last three teaching observations.
- Worked with Functional Skills co-ordinator to successfully implement and teach on the new Functional Skills ICT course, with a 100% pass rate.
- Recreated and ran the Alcohol Awareness course ensuring all barriers to learning where met efficiently and all information was current to meet set standards and criteria.
- Successful manageress of a retail shop for 10 years. The day-to-day running of a retail shop, including staffing, wage costs and budgeting, stocktaking, promoting goods and customer care.

KEY SKILLS

- Gained QTLS through continual professional development.
- Excellent knowledge of Microsoft Word, Excel, PowerPoint, Publisher and Database.
- Maintain professional standards and keep knowledge current through IFL Professional Development
- Equality and Diversity Level 2, Financial Capabilities Level 3
- Excellent disposition to offer and promote soft skills and motivation to diverse learners.
- Excellent sickness record; 0 days absent within the last 5 years and 3 days absent within the last 14 years.

CAREER HISTORY
Employability Tutor
Training Provider - 19/07/2011 – Present
Working with unemployed individuals to gain employment skills; soft skills (communication and confidence), CVs and interview skills.

ITQ Course Tutor
The Manchester College - Offender Learning
02/03/2006 – 18/07/2011
Fully co-ordinated, implemented and delivered ITQ from E3 to Level 2; assisted the implementation and creation of Functional ICT.

I.T Lecturer
Wakefield College - 08/10/2005 - 10/03/2006
Supported teaching assistants require and recognise ways of delivering and differentiating topics within ICT.

Warehouse Operative
Argos Distribution Centre - 11/04/1999 - 11/04/2006
Warehouse Operative

EDUCATION AND QUALIFICATIONS
A1 Assessor – in house training from The Manchester College - 2011
QTLS – Through IFL - 05/03/2010
Certificate in Education (Cert Ed) – Huddersfield University Level 5/6 - 06/06/2008
Transforming Learning with Information Learning Technology Level 4 Subject Specialism - 28/12/2005
JEB Diploma in ICT Practice and Principles Level 3 - 02/06/2005
Learning to Teach Online (Lettol) – Level 3 - 06/02/2006
Adult Numeracy Level 2 - 10/12/2009
Adult Literacy Level 2 – 15/03/2009
Advanced ECDL Word Level 3 - 27/02/2004
ECDL Level 2 - 03/09/2003
NVQ Customer Services Level 3 - 09/09/1996

PERSONAL INFORMATION
I have a bubbly and outgoing personality to which I feel has helped me achieve the success I have gained within Offender Learning. I have continued with this success within the employability sector by been a major part of our clients success. I believe in people and take huge satisfaction from the learners' comments on their progress. I am always willing to help others to progress and realise their own potential.

And there you have it, a step by step guide to your C.V. Before I move onto another session there are first some other things I need to go over with you. Look at the layout I have used. Try basing your C.V with a simple but effective layout. Use at least point 11 or 12 and the font should be something simple on the eye; such as Arial. Only use **bold** for sub headings.

Don't Go With The Flow

I just need to point out that under your key skills/achievements /strengths, really try and add at least one sentence to back up what you are saying. To just say that you are an excellent communicator is getting quite boring, so add another sentence or a few more words to stop it sounding like everybody else's. Okay, you're a team player who uses own initiative; bored bored bored; give me a sentence that really stands out. You can solve problems too I bet? Right, give a basic example. Anything is better than just writing it down.

Take a look at your C.V have you gone overboard on your background information? Take some out because you will get the chance to inform them of this at your interview.

Or can you word it better? Determined, decisive and can use own initiative to resolve problems and seek solutions. Sounds much better than: Can work on own initiative.

So there you go, we have covered the C.V, now you need to practice creating your own. Use mine as a guide, or you could look at the internet to view other samples.

I really could go on and on, about what you can put down on your C.V, but do the homework and you will find the answer. I am just helping you to develop your skills.

YOUR PASSPORT TO EMPLOYMENT

I cannot stress enough how important it is that you stand out for the right reasons, not the wrong ones. Take another look at your C.V and put yourself in the position of the employer. Say to yourself:

"Right, I have £15,000 to offer the right candidate. Would I offer me that role going on what I have read in the C.V?"

You need to be totally honest. If you wouldn't give yourself a job from reading your C.V, then you can bet an employer is thinking the same. So keep looking at your C.V, ask somebody else to be brutally honest with you. If it needs changing then do it.

"Remember, you should have one C.V for one job. Five different C.Vs for five jobs. Never have one C.V for numerous jobs."

RE-CAP AND CONSOLIDATION

So now do you understand why your C.V is so important? I know this section is very long and there is a lot to remember but re-read any part that you don't feel confident with.

The main part of the C.V is for it to stand out, use the keywords (a bank of keywords has been prepared for you) to ensure you stand out from the crowd. Realise what your *skills* are. Be positive and confident about your C.V; don't be scared that you're '*bragging*' because you're not. Other people going for the same job will be doing just the same.

So re-cap, (hope you haven't forgot it already):

✓ Research the job or company for aims, values, goals and mission statements and then edit your C.V to fit these
✓ Get the employer interested in you within just over half a page
✓ Have an appropriate e-mail address
✓ Keep the style simple and consistent
✓ Have a continuous timeline
✓ Proof-read your address
✓ Be prepared to give an example of everything on your C.V
✓ Use key words in your profile
✓ Recognise your skills and abilities
✓ Shout out about what you can do, don't advertise what you can't
✓ Get somebody else to read it to you
✓ Don't just put that you can *communicate,* or that you are a *team player.* It's boring, so tweak it so that it stands out more.

YOUR PERSONAL NOTE PAGE

In the space below, write down any thoughts, ideas and notes you feel will help you throughout the book.

_____

_____

_____

_____

_____

_____

_____

_____

_____

_____

_____

_____

_____

_____

_____

_____

_____

95

STEP 3

COVER LETTERS

AIM:	Develop, implement and understand how to create cover letters
OBJECTIVES:	By the end of this session you will be able to:

- ✓ Identify the importance of a cover letter.
- ✓ Create a cover letter.
- ✓ Use keywords from the job advert.
- ✓ Format the cover letter.
- ✓ Send your C.V and cover letter off with confidence.
- ✓ Understand the cover letters job.

Not to be mistaken for spec letters, we will cover those later on.

So what is a cover letter? This letter is to introduce yourself to a company with who you are sending your C.V off to. Many companies do not accept C.Vs without a covering letter. It is your introduction of yourself.

The cover letter is what an employer will look at before they even think about reading your C.V.

In my experience a cover letter may be just the one thing they read about you. How well you write a cover letter is very important, this letter is an example of how well you communicate. Most employers are not going to hire someone who they feel cannot write a perfect, error free cover letter. First impressions last, make your cover letter a great first impression.

A way in which I explain to the learners the difference between *cover* and *spec* letter is the following:

Cover Letters	Job Advertised
Spec Letters	No Job Advertised

10 ESSENTIAL COVER LETTER TIPS

I have listed below some tips to take into account when creating your cover letter:

1. What is the company about? Do your research.
2. Don't use *big* words to try and impress.
3. Try and get the contact details of the person you should send your letter to.

98

4. Don't ramble on; remember your introducing yourself to them and your C.V.
5. Keep a positive attitude when writing.
6. *Proof read*, this is the common mistake I find. Get somebody else to look through your letter for you.
7. Type your letter where available. I know that not everybody can use the computer but a typed up cover letter looks more professional.
8. Remain respectful when writing, it can be easy to 'slag' your boss off.
9. Try to make your letter stand out. Look at the job advertisement, what skills are they looking for?
10. Don't rest your coffee on the cover letter!

I would recommend you do a rough copy first. Read it out loud, criticise yourself if you need to. Be *'self aware';* be *'critical'*, if it sounds rubbish it probably is. So start again. Point 10 happened with one of the learners. I was proof reading it for her and I could not believe she was going to send it with coffee stains on it.

1 MAJOR COVER LETTER WARNING

It is really important that you put down the person's name you are writing to. Imagine you are working in an office or other environment. A cover letter and C.V land on your desk, there is no name or contact details on; who should it go to?

In many cases the letter and C.V will end in the *bin*, or under a pile of paperwork. The reason is this; if it does not concern the person who has the C.V and letter they will disregard it. There's no emotion towards you and your search for work.

So phone the company up and ask them for a specific name and/or department to where you should send your C.V/cover letter and/or application form.

99

HOW TO WRITE SUCCESSFUL ONLINE COVER LETTERS

You may have already experienced online application forms (more later), but quite often you are asked to send your C.V and cover letter through the companies online recruitment source. You will normally be asked to *'upload'* your C.V and write your cover letter from scratch. Okay, that's fine, but this is where you need to focus and carefully type away. You need to have a rough copy written down; you need to have researched the company. Don't just see a job advertised and write some words then add your C.V (like I have done!). You need to take extra time. Once you have done all of this you are ready to select *keywords*. Yes, as I have mentioned earlier these keywords are the words in which recruiters and the computers select your application forms – they are picking up your keywords. I will let you into a sneaky secret how to do this more effectively later on.

WHERE DO YOU GET THE KEY WORDS FROM?

The job description and company research, this is where you need to look. Gain knowledge of the company and edit and change your C.V/cover letter slightly. But focus on what their *'ideal candidate'* would have. I mentioned earlier that I had completed my cover letter without much thought. I was fed up of writing; I had uploaded my C.V and just droned on about my skills.

Nothing out of the ordinary. I was proper fed up; nobody had got back in touch. How inconsiderate. Now I do realise that my C.V would have just melted into the background along with many others. Because most online facilities are scanned by a computer, if there's no keywords then it's a no thank you. Lesson learnt for me is to take time and spend time on the research (yes I know I keep saying it), so the next two jobs I applied for I took the advice I have given you. Was I successful? I would look pretty foolish to ramble on if I weren't. Yes I got an interview for both. I declined one interview as I had then been offered other employment.

100

So before you upload it, grab some paper and a pen and scribble away about what they are looking for. See what the company values and future aims are etc.

Letter on I will give away a fantastic secret to help you stand out even more.

THE LAYOUT OF YOUR COVER LETTER

The layout of your cover letter should have at least 3/4 paragraphs. I have left space between each paragraph for you to write any details of jobs/companies in the future. I would copy out these four paragraphs or type them for future reference.

1. Which job are you applying for? Where was it advertised? Is there a job reference number?

2. What have you got to offer the company? What's your experience? Have you reached any targets etc?

3. Give a brief view of your knowledge on the company (mission statement, values and goals and explain how you can help the company reach these goals?

4. The end paragraph should be along the lines of when/how they can reach you and repeat how you are interested in the post.

101

A SAMPLE COVER LETTER WHICH WORKS TIME AND TIME AGAIN

Job Advert

Shop 'til' U Drop – Sales Assistant
Experienced and flexible individual
required. Excellent communication
skills and a passion for people are
essential to this job role.

Please send your C.V and Cover
Letter to Mr D Sachs, Job Ref:
092929

Ms T Clegg
22 Shepherds Way
Didsbury
NN6 8UJ

Email: t.c@hotmail.co.uk
Mobile: 8989898989898989898

Date: 00/00/00

Mr D Sachs
Recruitment Manager
Publisher Limited
Locks Lane
Northamptonshire
NN7 6YH

Dear Mr Sachs

Job Ref: 092929

I am writing in regards to the job vacancy advertised in the Northern Gazette on the 00/00/00. Please find my C.V/application form which gives you an indication of the skills I have to offer.

I am an experienced sales assistant with an adaptable and flexible attitude towards my work. I have outstanding communication skills which I use to maximise the strength of the company and to ensure customers return again and again. I am passionate about going that extra mile as I always get a sense of achievement.

I have looked at your mission statement and feel that I could be an excellent member of the team to help you achieve the mission statement and would be dedicated in helping push the company forward.

I would like to have the opportunity to meet you to discuss my application form further as I feel that I have the values and qualifications your company is looking for.

Yours Faithfully

Ms T Clegg

CHEEKY WAYS THAT WORK

Can you see what I have done with the cover letter? I have taken keywords from the job ad and tailored my cover letter to meet the requirements the employers are looking for.

Important: *This is where you will also tailor your C.V to fit the keywords into your Personal Profile.*

So in effect, you are exactly what the company is looking for. How smart is that? But again, I will repeat myself; it's no good manipulating and tailoring your C.V/cover letter if you really do not think you have the skills in the first place. You may just fall apart at the interview.

IF YOU THINK THIS IS A TWO MINUTE JOB – FORGET IT

Look at the third paragraph:

"I have looked at your mission statement and feel that I could be an excellent member of the team to help you achieve the mission statement and would be dedicated in helping push the company forward."

Before you apply for any job role, take the time to look at the company background. What are they about? What do they hope to achieve? What is their mission statement? What are their values? Do they have a particular aim? You can get a range of information about them if you do more research. You would be looking at around 1 hour to apply for one job. I have often taken longer. You need to research, edit and tailor your C.V and cover letter. Then proof read again. If you're doing this within 20-30 minutes then you're not spending enough time on the application process. So have a think, when was the last time you had an interview? If you're not hearing back from companies, then maybe this is why.
We will cover more about this within the Interview Sessions. But finding out about the company will harm you with *excellent knowledge* and you will *impress* the prospective employer. The extra time researching the company could be your *'ammunition'* to stand out from the rest.

103

Points To Consider So Your C.V And Cover Letter Works For You

You want to stand out from the crowd. You need to do the following as a rule of thumb before you attempt to send of your application form:

- ✓ Don't rush, take your time.
- ✓ Research the company.
- ✓ Ask yourself; "how can I add value?"
- ✓ Be confident in your writing tone, but don't come across as arrogant.
- ✓ Check that you know 'where' and 'who' to send the cover letter and C.V to.
- ✓ Use positive keywords; take them from the job advertised or their internet page.
- ✓ Get somebody else to look through it. Even e-mail it a friend or colleague so they can give their verdict. Tell them to be brutally honest with you.

Remember, using keywords are fantastic, but you must know and understand what these words actually mean. Take another look at this section before moving on to the next so that you know this bit inside and out.

RE-CAP AND CONSOLIDATION

In this section we have looked at how to create a cover letter. This session is not as long as the C.V building session because the cover letter is an introduction to you and your C.V.

But remember, look at the job advert. What skills and experiences are they looking for? Tailor your C.V and cover letter so that you are moulding yourself into that position. Do some extra homework and gain knowledge about the company.

Companies can be egotistical (like to hear good things about themselves). Don't go overboard with this though; you don't want to come across as a slimy snake. So think of one sentence that would sum up how you can add value.

Ask yourself, "Could I see myself working here?" If you could then you need to ask yourself, "What qualities can I bring." Have you heard that they are a good company to work for? Do you love their staff loyalty? What attracted you to the company in the first place?

YOUR PERSONAL NOTE PAGE

In the space below, write down any thoughts, ideas and notes you feel will help you throughout the book.

_____

_____

_____

_____

_____

_____

_____

_____

_____

_____

_____

_____

_____

_____

_____

_____

YOU HAVE THE SKILLS; NOW LEARN TO DEVELOP THEM

STEP 4

SPEC LETTERS

AIM:	Develop, create and understand the meaning of Spec Letters
OBJECTIVES:	By the end of this session you will be able to: ✓ Identify the importance of a spec letter. ✓ Create a spec letter. ✓ Format the spec letter. ✓ Use researching techniques. ✓ Build confidence with the speculative approach.

In short a spec letter is when there is no job advertised! Yes that's right, there is no job vacancy but you are still going to write to specific companies to which you will target.

So what's the point? Well, this speculative approach has a number of positives and a couple of negatives.

POSITIVES	NEGATIVES
Shows motivation	The cost of postage if you send your details via the post
Uses own initiative	Rejection
Displays a determined individual	
Actively seeking employment/progression/career change	
Put out your C.V before anyone else	
Place yourself inside the mind of the employer	
Confident and driven	

Even if the company which you are targeting does not want anybody at the moment, who is to say that you will make such a good impression that they may contact you in the future!

THE EMPLOYERS VIEW ON THE SPEC APPROACH

I have listed the positives and negatives of this approach to securing employment, but what do prospective employers get out of this?

If you're somebody who the company would normally be looking for, then this approach would save them time and money.

Here's how:

- No weekly job advert fee (*although an advert may still need to be placed*).
- No need to filter through hundreds of C.V's.
- Staff can focus on other priorities.
- Get a *'feel'* for you due to your approach.
- Know that you're driven to succeed not fail.
- Get a good first impression of you (unless you send your C.V and spec letter in that has got coffee stains etc on it).

So there are only positives to gain through this approach. But I am aware that using this approach takes confidence. How many of us have the ability and sell ourselves in this way? Sadly not many I can tell you.

When I first used this approach I felt 'cheeky', as though I was begging for a job. I soon realised that by changing the way I thought about this approach, the easier it was. I looked at it as though I was doing them a favour. I was promoting myself to them, cutting out the middle man; again a very hard thing to do for most of us.

Before you use the speculative approach I must stress that it is important that you research the targeted company before hand. Have a look at their values aims and/or mission statement. Using this approach takes time and effort but quite often it's worth it.

THE KEY TO EFFECTIVE RESEARCHING

Target Research Exercise

I have given you a few popular High Street names to research. If you don't have the internet why not try your local library and use their online facilities. After all, it's free. Don't under value the importance of this exercise. Believe me; I know that all you want is to get to the end of the book, with all of your skills. Remember I mentioned a process at the beginning? Well this is part of that process.

So search for:

1. Sainsbury's Supermarket
2. Boots
3. Greggs (the bakers)
4. Coca Cola
5. Primark

Find out what they are about. I have chosen these because the area of employment ranges vastly from sales assistant, team leaders/managers to warehouse operatives.

What information did you get? Did you have to look far? Yes, sometimes you may have to look around their website for a while, I always go their 'about us' section. There is usually useful information here.

The above are just examples; try looking at any company to see what additional information you can get. Maybe companies that you frequently use or have used in the past. It's all about knowledge remember?
I want you to get into the habit of researching every company you apply to. Yes I mean every company. Get the information and work with it. Use it on your C.V and Cover/Spec letters. This is one way how to stand out from the crowd and an effective way too.

110

IMPORTANCE OF: AIMS, VALUES, GOALS AND MISSION STATEMENTS

So how did you do? What did you find out about the company? How long did it take you? Is it worth going that bit further to make yourself stand out?

Hopefully you will have found out the following:

1. Sainsbury's Supermarket

Our values
Our five values provide the framework for how we do business at Sainsbury's. They guide us in everything we do - from key business decisions to day-today activities.

For us, retailing is about more than quality products and great service. It's also about supporting and helping the communities where we work, and being a good neighbour. We aim for our stores to be at the heart of the communities they serve.

2. Boots

Our customers are at the heart of our business. We're committed to providing exceptional customer and patient care, be the first choice for pharmacy and healthcare, offer innovative products 'only at Boots', with great value our customers love.

Our people are our strength and they tell us that Boots is a great place to work. We aim to always be the employer of choice, attracting and retaining the most talented and passionate people.

3. Greggs (*the bakers*)

Greggs began as a family business and we have retained our good, honest family values as the business has grown.

Our values are our commitment to the way we will treat each other. We aspire to be a company that everyone is proud to shop with, work for

111

and do business with. Our values apply to all our stakeholders, including our customers, our people, our shareholders and our suppliers.

4. Coca Cola

Our mission is:

To refresh the world - in mind, body and spirit.
To inspire moments of optimism - through our brands and actions.
To create value and make a difference everywhere we engage.

Our shared values that we are guided by are:

- Leadership
- Passion
- Integrity
- Accountability
- Collaboration
- Innovation
- Quality

5. Primark

We aim to make our employees, suppliers and local and wider communities' part of our success by working with them in every way we can. This means that:

- employees have equal opportunities based on merit
- suppliers are treated fairly
- local communities are respected and supported by Primark
- the company takes its environmental responsibilities seriously

Ask yourself this question. Has it hurt you in doing the research? Have you gained more knowledge? This simple process and often forgotten about approach could be the answer to getting your C.V and letters read.

Now ask yourself this question. Are you going to do this for every job you intend to apply for? If you have said to yourself "no" then re-read the book again. It is your responsibility to get this knowledge. Take ownership and get it!

Often these values, aims and mission statements are not advertised on the first web page, you have to search for them. They can usually be found at the bottom of a page under; *About Us*.I could find a lot more information about each of the above companies, but as I mentioned earlier you need to *'take ownership'* and find out as much information as you can.

So what do you do with this information?

The first thing you do is add parts of the information into your **spec letter and your C.V**. The second thing is to use this information for when you have an interview (covered later).

On the following pages I have given you examples of spec letters and how I would format and word the letter to two of the above companies.

THE SPECULATIVE APPROACH THAT REALLY WORKS

Sample Spec letter 1

Ms T Clegg
22 Shepherds Way
Didsbury
NN6 8UJ

Email: t.c@hotmail.co.uk
Mobile: 8989898989898989898

Date: 00/00/00

Head of Recruitment
Boots – Chemist
123 Roll Road
Didlington
DD8 4TG

Dear Sir or Madam (unless you know a specific name)

I am writing to enquire whether you have any vacancies within your company, or which may be arising in the future. My experience has been within the customer care/sales assistant role.

I hugely believe in your products and feel that your level of customer service is second to none, having been one of your loyal customers for a number of years. I feel that with my excellent people skills and understanding nature I can help your company continue with the exceptional customer care it is proud of.

I am an experienced sales assistant with an adaptable and flexible attitude towards my work. I have outstanding communication skills which I have used to maximise the strength of the company and to ensure customers return again and again. I am passionate about going that extra mile as I always feel a sense of achievement.

Please find enclosed a copy of my C.V and I would like to take this opportunity to thank you for your time and look forward to hearing from you in the future.

Yours Faithfully

Ms T Clegg

114

Sample Spec Letter 2

Ms T Clegg
22 Shepherds Way
Didsbury
NN6 8UJ

Email: t.c@hotmail.co.uk
Mobile: 8989898989898989898

Date: 00/00/00

Head of Recruitment
Coca Cola Ltd
123 Roll Road
Didlington
DD8 4TG

Dear Sir or Madam (unless you know a specific name)

I am writing to enquire whether you have any vacancies within your company, or which may be arising in the future.

I have worked within the role as a warehouse operative for numerous years and feel that I have the passion, quality and integrity as mentioned in your values to help the company achieve their mission statement and to be continually guided by the shared values.

I am a self motivated individual who always strives to deliver a high standard of service within any role I undertake. Playing part of a team has been a significant part of my previous success in reaching and often exceeding targets set.

Please find enclosed a copy of my C.V and I would like to take this opportunity to thank you for your time and look forward to hearing from you in the future.

Yours Faithfully

Ms T Clegg

Do A Bit Of Butt Kissing

So what's your first thought? Well I will let you into a secret; I cringed with embarrassment when I first sent out my spec letter.

When I deliver this session to the learners I can see the look of fear on their faces. I say to them, *"basically, you're kissing their backsides."* It is at this moment that I know that they feel uncomfortable with the prospect of sending out a spec letter.

At the beginning of this session within the objectives, I stated that one objective would be to become confident when using the *speculative approach*. So the first thing you need to do is look at the local paper or on the internet to find any job vacancy. Once you have done this, practice looking for their values, aims and/or mission statements.

What you need to do here is think about the other people going for this job; you need to stand out from them. So get yourself harmed with ammunition. This ammunition is your knowledge of the company.

Take it step by step; start off with targeting one company. Do your research and then send off your spec letter with your C.V.

As I mentioned earlier, the negatives of this approach is the cost of sending your C.V and spec letter out. This is something that could be overcome; maybe ask an advisor at the Job Centre (if you claim JSA) to give you envelopes and stamps. If you're not on JSA then find the money yourself. You're only talking a couple of pounds here.

The other negative I mentioned is the *rejection*. Nobody likes to be rejected and I am sure we have all been there at some point; either within employment area or within our personal lives.

So the trick here is not to take it too personally if you don't hear anything. Remember there is no job, your just trying your luck, using your own initiative.

116

One learner said to me during one of these sessions:

"Tracey, I don't see the point of this approach. I sent out at least 90 – 100 Spec letters with my C.V and only got one job offer." This is what I wanted to hear. He got a job offer, which is the whole point of the speculative approach. I went on to mention that he would not have got that if he hadn't done it this way.

THE GOLDEN RULE BEHIND HANDING OUT YOUR C.V'S

Okay, I have covered you sending or even e-mailing your C.V to the targeted companies, but what about going around your local area, areas of interest to you and asking to speak to the manager. You will then introduce yourself briefly and give him your spec letter and C.V.

I know my first reaction and feeling. Scared, nervous and feeling quite daft. The thought of it does still make me feel nervous. But it is an excellent way of getting yourself out there.

So what first impressions do you need to give off?

Scenario exercise

You are walking around your High Street or main City Centre to hand out your C.V and spec letter.

What do you need to do or consider? Have a think and write your thoughts down in the space (or on a separate sheet of paper).

117

Things to take into account:

_____

_____

_____

_____

_____

What did you come up with? At this point, I must mention that I am not trying to teach you how to suck eggs or patronise you. It's just sometimes we under-estimate what people are thinking, what we may look like.

So things to take into account when personally handing out your spec letter and C.V are:

- ✓ Dress smart, dress as though you are going for an interview. This is the first time you will be meeting a 'could be potential employer'.

- ✓ Look at your hands, are they clean? Are they free from chipped nail polish?

- ✓ Are your shoes or trainers clean and free from dirt?

- ✓ Are your clothes fresh, clean and ironed?

118

✓ Smile, be confident and polite.

✓ Use your excellent communication skills.

✓ Make sure your C.V and spec letter are printed to a high standard on quality paper, as opposed to on creased up paper.

We have all heard about first impressions and how they last, well remember this each time you use the speculative approach.

A lot of effort I know. But if it could secure you a job, make you stand out from everybody else then so be it. Just do it. Another reason for using the speculative approach is that you will be seen as a motivated and determined individual who is working hard to gain employment or determined to change careers etc.

Basically you have nothing to lose. So think positive and be confident. You are doing the right thing; you may feel nervous or anxious by handing your letters out in person but again it's a confidence issue. You will benefit. My colleague informed me that her husband gained six job offers from using this speculative approach; one of those was 6 months after he had handed it to the manager as they kept his name on file.

On the next page I have added a *spec template*; you will need to alter certain details but the layout and some of the wording you could use. I have left blank spaces for you to fill in when you have researched the company and gained some useful information.

SPECULATIVE TEMPLATE FOR YOU TO USE

Simply re-type this adding your own information in the space below:

Shelly Baggins
23 Tripe Lane
Pontefract
North Midlands
NN8 9KL

Email: Phone:

Date: /   /

Dear Sir/Madam,

Please could I take this opportunity to introduce myself to you and to your company? I have attached my C.V which outlines my key skills, strengths and abilities and would appreciate your time in looking at the C.V for future reference should any suitable vacancies arise.

I am currently looking for employment within ---- Sector and having looked at your website I feel that I have the skills and knowledge to help you achieve your aims of ---.   .

I can add value to your company (State a brief sentence on how you can add value). My experience has been ---, to which I have helped the company in reaching targets and goals (if you can, then give specifics).

Thank you very much for your time and I look forward to hearing from you in the future.

Yours Faithfully
Shelly Baggins

RE-CAP AND CONSOLIDATION

So what have we taken from this session? Hopefully, you will realise that using the *speculative approach* is a worthwhile task. Again, look at it from an employer's point of view, look at the *confidence, determination, motivation* and *self-belief* you're advertising about yourself. Look how *'pro active'* you come across. If you're un-employed at the moment then I am sure that your advisor at the Job Centre has already spoken to you about this approach. If you are in work, then this is a great way of *'getting yourself out there'*. Test the water; see what career path/progression or promotion there is.

You need to do this for every company you are targeting. Even those that have been advertising for job vacancies. Use the keywords you have found and edit and tailor your C.V and letters to suit. Obviously, you must feel *confident* with how you tailor your C.V and letters. Really mean what you are saying; really mean that you can actually carry out what you are promising.

Scrutinise the company, get as much information as you can. Make the effort upfront then this will pay off. Lastly, take a look at yourself. Could you do with smartening up a bit? Do you need to have a good wash? Be self aware and really dress for the part (I will cover first impressions later).

IMPORTANT TASK BEFORE SENDING OFF YOUR SPEC LETTER

Research the companies first, look at their:

- VALUES
- AIMS
- MISSION STATEMENTS
- VISION FOR THE FUTURE

121

YOUR PERSONAL NOTE PAGE

In the space below, write down any thoughts, ideas and notes you feel will help you throughout the book.

_____

_____

_____

_____

_____

_____

_____

_____

_____

_____

_____

_____

_____

_____

_____

_____

_____

_____

STEP 5

EFFECTIVE JOB SEARCHING

AIM:	Identify effective ways to job search.
OBJECTIVES:	By the end of this session you will be able to:

- ✓ Understand effective job searching tools.
- ✓ Recognise different jobsites and C.V libraries.
- ✓ Develop your own job searching skills and techniques.

Within this short session I will help you to develop your job searching techniques. You may think that you know how to job search, but I am going to give you *my* tips.

Also within this section it is quite important that you get used to using the internet to search for jobs. Whether you use somebody else's computer (Library, JCP, Local Clubs, friends etc), it is extremely important that you get used to looking *online*. Many jobs now are only advertised this way.

It may be that you need ICT (computer lessons) to be able to feel confident enough with using the computer. Don't let this be a barrier, if you're out of work and claiming JSA, there are loads of courses free. Use it, get as much as you can while searching for work. Go to your local library or community centre and I'm pretty sure they will be bursting with advice for you. I know my local community centre is a haven for many people and there are such a wide range of courses for you to enrol on.

DO YOU NEED A KICK UP THE BACKSIDE?

Can you honestly say that you put 100% effort into job searching? Could you do more?

I ask this question to every learner I meet, they are quite honest and tell me: *"I suppose I could do more, it's just that I have got into the habit of scanning the internet and that's it."*

Dam right, many of you could do more, I know it can be time consuming, or if you're doing it wrong it won't be. But searching for jobs online can take hours, especially if you're doing it right.

I do understand that many people lose faith in ever finding a job, but I promise you that if you put the effort in and take my advice throughout this book then you will get that job interview and hopefully the job. Remain positive, even when you're thinking, *"What's the point?"* You will get there.

HOW TO GET ON THE EMPLOYMENT LADDER

YOUR FIRST 2 STEPS TO FINDING A JOB

Here is a start up guide I want you to make sure you are doing, if not get it done as soon as.

1. Once you are completely happy with your C.V get it registered at on an online CV library such as 'Monster.co.uk' *(useful web addresses later)*. This can be quiet a lengthy process, but you really must take your time and be patient.

2. Set yourself an email alert from jobsites (make sure you're email is appropriate) and check your emails regularly. Your local Job Club can set you up with an email address account. Lists of useful jobsites come later. I still have email alerts registered and I actually get some of them when they first appear.

It is really important that each time you add qualifications or additional details to your C.V then make sure you re-register your new C.V. Write down your password to these sites to make logging in easier.

Whether you are claiming JSA or not, make sure you look at the '*Direct Gov*' site regularly, this is because many of the jobs advertised on there are gone in a short space of time. Utilise your time wisely and get looking before dinner time because many of the jobs are already taken. But don't just rely on this as the only source of vacancies. Look at the other job sites at the end of the book.

But don't keep telling yourself, *"There are no jobs out there."* Yes there are, you need to find them. Nobody is going to come to you with a handful of job offers. Take responsibility. It can work, honestly.

Within one of the companies I worked for we needed a new member of staff. After 8 months we finally got to interview a suitable candidate. Eight months of advertising and it wasn't even a high profile role or team leader position either.

So get it out of your head that there are no jobs. Yes there are, you may just need to put more effort in.

IF IN DOUBT, USE A SEARCH ENGINE

Many people who I have helped have struggled to use job searching to its fullest potential. Either because they have limited ICT experience or get fed up after 30 minutes. Persevere, get comfy and spend at least double your usual time on job searching.

If you don't know any of the main jobsites (more later), type into the search engine what you are looking for. Look at the example below:

> Searching for warehouse work in Ossett, West Yorkshire

This is your first step to filtering out a job. Obviously you will key in the words which are relevant to you. You will then be presented with pages of information, some useful and some random rubbish. You just need to keep wading through the website, and don't just keep to one because you're familiar with it. Look at the list of job sites you're presented with, over 11,000 were found when I searched for jobs in Ossett, West Yorkshire. Like I said earlier, I have a naughty little secret to share with you at the end of the book.

THERE'S A JOB, NOW WHAT?

Let's just say that you have found a job advertised working as a 'Customer Advisor' for B & Q. It says that you should attach your C.V and add a cover letter. So what do most people do? Rush in like 'a Bull in a China shop'. Honestly I have seen this so many times. Well stop it now.

The first thing you should do when applying for a job is to print off the advert. And if you are lucky the job advert will be full of *keywords* for you to nab (*pinch*).

126

Look at the advert below (I nabbed it from B & Q):

> For this role you will be required to have to the following attributes:

✓ An enthusiastic and energised attitude.
✓ A passion for delivering excellent customer service.
✓ Enjoy working with others as a team.
✓ Ability to work effectively without direct supervision.
✓ Ability to multi-task in a busy, fast paced environment.
✓ A passion for Home Improvement.
✓ Flexibility to cover store opening hours including. evenings, weekends and bank holidays on a rota basis
✓ A down to earth attitude and a friendly approach as well as a desire to help others and a willingness to learn are essential in this role.

So the second thing you should do is look to see if the above attributes are you, and if so, make sure they are on your C.V and on part of your Cover Letter.

What about the company? Have you researched their *value, aims* etc? Write down a couple of lines about what you have found on your form and C.V etc. Then you proof-read your work. Once you are happy with all of that, you can press **send** *(if it's an online process)*. This is exactly what you would do when using the *spec approach* too. But just remember to proof-read before you click send.

I cannot stress enough that you have got to do this with every single job you apply for. This is why it takes time when job searching effectively.

You Don't Have All The Skills, So What

Another mistake I come across is that people will just neglect a job advert because they don't have all of the necessary skills. So, you're not perfect are you? Don't let this put you off; by the time you have read this book, you will be more confident in applying for these jobs.

Let me give you an example, I once applied for a Team Leader role for the Princes Trust. I had no idea what this was about and I had never been a team leader. Guess what? I got an interview. I did actually phone them and say that I had already gained employment and thanked them for their time. But do you know what else? I used the same application form two months earlier to apply for another role (not team leader), exactly the same company. I received an email informing me that I was not successful in the application process. Amazing really when I had all, if not more qualifications for this job, yet they wanted to see me regarding another (*six grand diff too*). So just to make that clearer; if you have most of the skills advertised then go for it. What's the worst that could happen? An old colleague of mine also attended an interview for a team leader role; again it is something she is not familiar with. But they saw her soft skills, her enthusiasm and passion so they decided to employ her. How great is that? Look at the job role again, read what it says and have a good think about your experience. Can you relate to it even though you don't have qualifications in that area? Remember you can always '*sell*' the fact that you are a quick learner and that you are willing to be trained up in that field. This can be a positive point within some companies as they would much rather train an individual to their standards and use their own criteria which matches the company and what they do. Think about it. They train you to their needs, not you bringing in skills you learnt years ago with another company. Just don't rule any job out because you don't feel you have all the skills.

You've Got An Interview - Now What?

You research the company even more. That's what. I have already gone on about this, but just make sure you do it I will repeat myself. We will cover the interview in another session. You prepare yourself, you research the job description and you research their aims, values, goals and mission statements. But you must also look at your C.V; *know it, be it.*

You Have Not Been Successful

If you do happen to get a *rejection letter*, then what a surprise, but why don't you phone the company and ask for feedback on your application form? What harm is it going to do? This is called being 'pro-active'. The skill here is to try and not take the rejection to heart. I understand how hard it is, but they don't know you. They don't know how good you are, therefore, they don't deserve you as an employee. I now that's going overboard but if it helps. I can't stress enough how important this part is, get the feedback and work on it.

129

RE-CAP AND CONSOLIDATION

By now you should be realising that with every step of the process so far, you have been tailoring yourself to fit the job description. This is the key to getting *noticed* so far. When you search online for jobs you may also need to change *keywords* which you would normally use.

Try searching all jobs within your area (or areas you are willing to travel to). Again, this takes time, but if it gets you seeing the jobs then your time is worth it.

Usually, well in quite a few cases, what happens when you apply online is that there is a computer at the other end filtering through the application forms/C.Vs/Cover letters. Again, keywords are the key. If you manipulate your application form so that it more or less matches the job advert, you should be getting your forms looked at. Don't forget to look at the end of the book for tips on 'how to beat the computer filter'.

This is not to say that you will be successful, but at least you will know your hard work and time is paying off. One of these forms *will* get you an interview if you keep doing the *tweaking*.

Get up and about early to get a first look at prospective jobs. They may be gone by dinner time so get your preparation and application forms etc done quickly and get applying.

I will repeat myself again, look at the job description (as we have covered earlier) and if you need to apply online, then make sure you use the knowledge I have just shared with you – alter and tweak your form so that you *fit* in with what the company is looking for.

YOUR PERSONAL NOTE PAGE

In the space below, write down any thoughts, ideas and notes you feel
will help you throughout the book.

_____

_____

_____

_____

_____

_____

_____

_____

_____

_____

_____

_____

_____

_____

_____

_____

131

CONSOLIDATION OF STEPS 1 – 5

Phew, I go on a bit don't I?

Look at how much time you have spent looking at these sessions. This is because this is mainly the only way to secure a chance of employment through a great if not fantastic C.V, spec and cover letter.

Points to remember:

- Think about your **transferrable skills.**
- Don't use language you don't feel comfortable with.
- Don't use words you don't understand.
- Think long and hard about your **Personal Profile.**
- List your **key skills** and **achievements.**
- Keep the layout of your C.V consistent (same line spacing, font and size etc).
- Research the company before sending off your C.V, cover letter or spec letter.
- You should be able to **back up** everything that is on your C.V.
- Tailor your C.V and spec/cover letters to the needs of the job advertised or the job you are writing about.
- Be positive and dress smart, especially if you are walking around handing out your details.

So I will repeat myself again, look at the job description and see how you can use some of their advertising words within your C.V, cover/spec letter. Companies love being told how great they are, rub their ego. But one thing to remember throughout all of these exercises, the key is to believe in yourself too. You are worthy of a chance, you just need to prove it to the employers.

THE END FACT

You need to get out there and sell yourself. You need to be confident that you have skills, even if you feel you have not used them in a while. Put all of these skills together and already you become more employable, more likely to gain promotion.

Don't forget the fact that I am telling you all of this because I know what barriers many of you face. I know how difficult it can be to become motivated let alone to be positive about it too. But the bottom line is this:

"Stop blaming people for what you have not got and work hard to get it. You deserve a chance of employment or promotion. You have the skills, now learn to develop them."

"What have I got to lose?"

Tracey Morewood

C.V KEYWORDS

Below I have listed some key words which I recommend you look at. These words can make your C.V stand out from the crowd.

Achieved	Developed	Managed	Self-belief
Administered	Directed	Motivated	Self-motivated
Capable	Efficient	Organised	Enhance
Competent	Established	Planned	Collated
Communicated	Facilitated	Positive	Delegated
Co-ordinated	Implemented	Profitable	Generated
Created	Improved	Successful	Approved
Designed	Inspired	Evaluated	Coached
Proposed	Researched	Represented	Initiated
Negotiated	Observed	Promoted	Structured
Succeeded	Trained	Strengthened	Suggested
Founded	Applied	Budgeted	Customised
Defined	Identified	Influenced	Maintained
Led	Supervised	Won	

The above words are 'action' words; they show that you have used action in getting something done.

I must say that there are loads of other words to help you stand out from the crowd that can be found on the internet. But this book is not just about the C.V and the words to use. That could be a whole new book. If you do need other words then get on the web and search through it.

Remember

Make sure you feel comfortable with the words you choose on your C.V and cover /spec letters. Do you know what they mean? Can you explain them within an interview? Have you got evidence to back up your claim? By the time you have finished this book you will have.

Your C.V is YOU.

NOW FOR THE HARD BIT!

HOW TO GAIN POSITIVE THOUGHTS AND SELF BELIEF

If you thought the first part of the book was intense, then you are in for a right treat. Yes, I am been sarcastic. Within the next few sections I will be going more into *soft skills*.

Many of you may be thinking: "*I am not bothering about reading this part; it's nothing to do with me.*"

Or are you thinking: "*I think I am positive and I have got loads of confidence.*"

The word soft skill tends to put people off, usually men. This is not a sexist remark, but from my experience, and don't forget everything within this book is put down from my own experience and knowledge, not by using the internet. But men usually see these words and think; "*I'm okay ta, I don't need help in this area.*"

So I get them to come along and I guarantee that within one of the following sessions, they have learnt something. To this day not one person has said that they have thought it a waste of time. And believe me; I operate a fully honest and open policy regarding learners and their opinion on the learning journey. How does this link to becoming employable or even moving up the career ladder or changing careers?

If you are not too sure about how this links then I suggest you re-read the first part of this book. It's all about what employers want. It's about uncovering your often lost potential. It is about believing that you have something good to offer and believing in yourself. So let's crack on with the next bit.

STEP 6

POSITIVITY AND MOTIVATION –

WITH CONFIDENCE, SELF BELIEF AND SELF ESTEEM

AIM:	Recognise the importance of having a positive outlook and understand how confidence, self esteem and motivation can be linked to employability skills.
OBJECTIVES:	By the end of this session you will be able to:

    ✓ State own fears and barriers.

    ✓ Demonstrate self belief and esteem.

    ✓ Recognise importance of training your negative thoughts.

    ✓ Write down confidently the qualities you like about yourself.

    ✓ Become self-aware of your strengths/skills and goals you would like to achieve.

    ✓ State why these skills are wanted by employers.

139

When I start this session with my learners, I always apologise. Yes, I apologise for how I am probably going to come across. I didn't always feel comfortable in teaching this session, I felt as though I was *'preaching'* to the learner.

But like I stated earlier within the book, I will never teach anything I don't believe in myself. I truly believe that this topic is a major barrier to progression, to gaining employment and to changing careers.

In my view, around 98% of people I have met suffer with a lack of the above. I don't just mean on the course but in general. Many people, if they are honest with themselves often wear a mask. Me included. But deep down, many are scared of coming out of their comfort zone and talking about how great they are.

I teach through experience, as opposed to teaching from what the book or resources say I should teach.

Remember:

You may think you're not going to bother with this section, but *please* take my advice and at least read through it.

You may feel that you don't need support in this area. Okay, what have you got to lose?

Throughout the following pages and exercises there are no strict *right* or *wrong* answers. They are your views and opinions. This is part of the process of being '*self aware*'.

Exercise 1

In the space below, place a tick to which you feel represents your confidence level: (*one is low on confidence, 10 is very confident.*)

1	2	3	4	5	6	7	8	9	10

When I have done this previously, the learners need a lot of time, I ask them to *be honest*.

Why do you think that this is a hard task to do?

It's because we are not used to thinking deeply and honestly about how confident we are. We don't like putting 9 or 10 because as many people in my class say:

"*I don't really like putting a high score in case people think I am being big headed or something.*"

But the sad case is, not many put down more than 5 in my experience. With issues from previous experience within work, *put downs* from family members or friends or some other reason. Once we feel low on confidence it can be really hard to pick ourselves up from it.

Again, I speak from experience. When I decided to write my own *employability book,* I felt as though some people just *humoured* me. I felt as though people like me should concentrate on daily work life and leave book writing to somebody else.

So in all honestly, depending on the situation I was in, I would often place myself at a 4 or 5. I say to the learners; *"what would you place me at?"* And the same reply is given; 9 or 10. When I explain that yes, now I would place myself at this level on most days, but on others I would place my score a lot lower. This is because I get used to wearing a *mask.* I become louder to make me look more confident.

Again, this is something I am working on and I read a *'self help'* book; *"Feel the fear and do it anyway,"* *(*Susan Jeffers). I have many fears and barriers probably like you, but now I am doing something to overcome these. Let me tell you, the way in which we think can alter our lives. Deep, yes. But in my view so true.

THE IMPORTANCE OF SELF CONFIDENCE

This then leads me onto one of the most important skills you need to secure that job, promotion or career change. Have a look at the question below.

Why is self confidence important? Write down in the space below your opinions.

_____

_____

Self confidence in my view means one thing. *Self belief.* I believe so much in this skill, and sadly this is one of the things that many of us lack; me at times also. To have self-belief is to basically believe in yourself, your skills and what values you have. There is not one person on this earth that could say to me that they don't have anything good to offer.

142

Within my years within Offender Learning, this is one of the biggest things I would try and give to the learners. I still maintain the same view:

**"If we don't belief in ourselves, then nobody else will,
Push yourself and you will realise you can do anything."**

Tracey Morewood

I have come up against many obstacles and the most recent has been within my role as employability tutor. I have created, developed and delivered courses with limited information. I have wanted to sit and cry because I was taken out of my own *comfort zone*. So I brushed myself down, said to myself that there is nothing I cannot achieve, I can achieve anything I put my mind to. Let me tell you, this is hard. But I refuse to be beaten without a fight (again, I think this is the Yorkshire lass in me).

So even when I have felt that I cannot carry on, I always tell myself; "*you can do it.*" I know it's not easy, so don't think I have had an easy life, everything coming up roses, far from it. But I have developed a huge sense of *self belief*. This skill, and let me tell you it is a skill which doesn't come naturally to the majority of people, me included. You need to tell yourself each day that you can do anything you put your mind to.

You *can* add *value* to any prospective employer.

I always give examples to learners' about my own obstacles and barriers. I feel it is important that they fully understand that, even though they may look at me when I am teaching and think that I am full of confidence, deep down I really try and overcome any *negative* emotions and thoughts by telling myself that:

"*Do you know what, I can do this, and I will try my hardest to do so. If it doesn't go how I planned then so what; I tried my best.*"

MAKE AFFIRMATIONS WORK FOR YOU

MY OWN PERSONAL THOUGHTS

This leads me onto *affirmations,* and when I delivered a session on self-esteem and positivity, I explained what these were. I then did a consolidation exercise and I asked one member of the group, "*What is an affirmation?*" Their reply was:

> "*It's one of them reet good sentences that sound dead nice.*"

I thought to myself that I couldn't have put it any better myself. I am not going to go on too much about affirmations, but I have just put down two of my favourite, which I feel many of you will relate to:

WHAT LIFE DEALS ME I HAVE THE STRENGTH TO GET THROUGH IT

I may have feared many things, but I have gained a huge amount of self-belief which helps me handle anything. I now know that fear only exits because I allow it to. I now understand that I am worthy of success choose how small. When I speak I don't feel foolish, I am just as important as the next person. I can handle any stresses in life and I will learn from each opportunity that I am faced with. I understand that rejection will make me stronger; I will not give up until I have achieved my goal.

I CAN'T BLAME ANYONE FOR THE DOWNFALLS IN MY LIFE: EXCEPT ME

I may moan about things in my life but are they really that bad? I have the strength to change that. I can choose to listen to the negative comments of others and feed off their negative thoughts or I can choose to be more positive with my own thoughts. I can play the 'victim' or I can get off my backside and take responsibility for my life. If I want to better myself then there is only one person stopping me. That is me.

Tracey Morewood

144

Now, originally I was going to use two affirmations from the self help book I mentioned earlier. Then I thought about it and came to the conclusion that it's mad me putting somebody else's work here. I will put down what I think each day to often get me through hard times.

POSITIVITY BREEDS POSITIVITY

The above two are what I say to myself each day; positive thoughts can bring positive outcomes. What are you thinking as you read this? Honestly, if you're having negative thoughts then so did I. When I explain to people how much I have changed in myself and my outlook on life is very positive their eyes seem to roll as though they think I am some do-gooder who is preaching.

You could not be further from the truth. I have had many put downs over the years and believe me I felt as though I was the *'victim'*. I then realised that I would always be the victim if I allowed it. I have become much stronger inside and this is through self belief. Like I mentioned, I still use these positive thoughts as part of my every day routine.

As mentioned earlier in the book, I only teach what I believe my learners will benefit from. Even those young, cool, *'bit of an attitude'* learners will always say to me;

"I thought you were going to preach to us or something, but when you actually look at the words and listen to what you're saying I think you're right."

That is when I know I have had a break-through. One learner said that when he attended meetings or interviews, he always felt paranoid. He felt as though nobody was interested in what he had to say. I said to him that this is where he needs to learn positive thoughts, and be strong to say in the correct way:

"This is my opinion on the subject."

145

He came back the week after and told me that he felt uncomfortable within a meeting; he felt that his opinions didn't count. That there were too many 'confident' characters in the room. He then decided to speak, to see if my words worked. He soon realised that he had been paranoid all along.

We have all heard the saying *'there's no such word as can't'*. It is quite easy to say *"I can't"*, but it is even easier to *"I can, because I will learn."* If you have children then I am sure you have even said the above to them; and if your children are *"Smart Alecs"* like mine they will have said:

"No mum, I cannot tidy my bedroom." The point here is that we are so quick to say that we cannot or can't do something, when in reality we can.

WHAT MAKES YOU FEEL UNCOMFORTABLE?

So let's move onto another small task. Here I want you to think about things or people which make you feel uncomfortable or lack confidence.

List 3 things or people which make you feel uncomfortable and maybe lack confidence:

1.

2.

3.

How did you do? Again, this question is so very hard for the majority of my learners. How many times are you asked to do the above task? Not very often I bet. But what this does is it makes you become more aware of what or who can make you feel like this.

146

Below I have given a list of answers from the learners (the odd one from me) taken over a period of time:

- My boss, line manager
- Other colleagues
- My parents, siblings, friends
- People who just look at me and judge me
- My teachers
- Partner/husband/wife
- School/college years

There have been other answers over time, but these are the most common ones I see on a daily basis. This really got me thinking, there are many people out there who feel intimidated by others. Feel worthless compared to others. Constant *'put downs'* have often chipped away at the individuals own self-esteem and belief to such a point that they doubt they have got anything good to offer anyone, let alone employers.

The thing is, I can see potential in every learner and fully believe that each learner has something to offer. One of my hardest jobs is to actually get the learner to believe in themselves. Eventually they would leave the course and each one will state that they have learnt. This would be another 'teary' moment for me!

So hopefully that has got you thinking more about yourself. I cannot stress enough how important it is to try and break down your barriers, whatever they may be. Try and think positive about each situation you are faced with, if you think negative all of the time, then surely negative things will happen.
Writing this book has taken me quite a long time, but my passion and belief has kept me motivated. But, what if nobody buys it? I have wasted all of my time on it, all of my energy. That would be the negative way of thinking, but how I think is that I have enjoyed doing it.

147

I believe in the book and what I do. I believe in myself and how I teach so I have enjoyed the journey so far.

I also think that I fully believe that this book could help so many people that I am going to work and work to ensure it gets published. The worst case scenario would be that all of my family and friends get the same gift for Christmas!

So we have looked at what things or people make you feel uncomfortable or lack confidence, but what are your strengths?

Think about what you are good at, what do you think are your strengths? I hope you're not rolling your eyes again at this! Okay, if you're struggling with this task, put yourself in the shoes of an employer, you are asking this question in an interview. What fantastic answers would you like to hear from the interviewee? I will give you some tips later on which I would expect to hear.

YOUR TOP 5 STRENGTHS

1. _____

2. _____

3. _____

4. _____

5. _____

Easy or hard? When I do this with the learners you can just see the look of despair on their faces, strength what strength? This is because again, they are not used to saying what they are good at. If you where to go out and do a survey to the public and asked them the same question, I bet the majority would struggle to answer.

It is rare that many individuals can find 5 strengths. Like most of us, they under-estimate their capabilities. They don't like to put it down in case they come across as *arrogant* or *cocky*.

148

So if you were asked this as an interview question (full interview techniques later) you would need to know this straight away. You would need to remember this so that you can speak fluently and confidently in an interview.

UNDERSTAND HOW POWERFUL AND STRONG YOU CAN BE

Right, I will ask you again. What are your 5 strengths?

I would love to hear some of the following:

- Natural ability to lead and motivate a team
- Ability to communicate effectively at all levels
- Passionate about inspiring others
- Kind and caring nature
- Willing to go out of your way for somebody
- Fantastic team player, always motivating others
- Enthusiastic
- Outstanding organisational skills
- A proven ability to hit and exceed targets
- Flexible and able to respond positively to change
- Adaptable to individual needs, caring and able to work using my own initiative
- Building and maintaining strong and effective relationships with customers

There are many more I know, but like I said I can go on a bit so I thought I would leave it to your imagination.

149

Don't worry if you didn't list any of those above, the important thing here is that you did actually find a strength. If you didn't, then you are *under-estimating* how good you are.

Never mind what other people think of your skills and strengths. What do you see as your strengths? This is where we let ourselves fall down, listening to what others say. I always say to the learner;

> **"If you're not going to blow your own trumpet about how good you are, the next person will most certainly be bragging about their own skills."**

Tracey Morewood

Look at this in an interview situation; the interviewer has asked you to tell them what you are good at. You sell yourself short, and a big fat cross will be placed on the interviewers' notes. How mad would you be at yourself? This is why you need to get used to *'bigging'* yourself up; selling yourself is crucial to gaining employment or progressing within your existing employment.

Now, on the list of strengths I have just given you, do they look familiar? I hope so; I listed most of these earlier within the C.V section. So why do you think this has got anything to do with employability skills? Because most of you will have at least one of these strengths on your C.V. Again, understanding what is on your C.V is important; it is your own personal glossy brochure.

NICK THE STRENGTHS, YOU HAVE THEM ANYWAY

Right, now for the cheeky bit!

What strengths are mentioned in the job advert below? This has been taken off the internet from an actual jobsite:

Retail Assistant Required

Making sure our customers get precisely what they need will be down to you. This means you'll be responsible for delivering everything from helpful advice about our clothing range to impactful in-store merchandising - with the help of our guidelines. Driving sales, delivery processing and stock replenishment will also be part and parcel of your role.

We're looking for confident self starters with real people skills, infectious enthusiasm and excellent problem-solving skills. If you have experience in a retail fashion or clothing environment too we would love to hear from you.

I will ask you again, from an interviewers' point of view; *"What strengths do you feel you have?"*

Have a think about how you would respond to this. Then the skill here what you are starting to develop are your *Interview responses*.

151

Now this is what I would say were my own strengths if I was to go for this particular job:

- ✓ Ability to meet the demands and needs of the customer
- ✓ Outstanding ability to meet targets
- ✓ Passion for people and understand the importance of going '*that extra mile*'
- ✓ Confident and self motivated
- ✓ Excellent problems solving skills
- ✓ Bubbly and enthusiastic nature
- ✓ Able to motivate others especially within teams

So this brings me back to the beginning, did you think I was going off track there? I usually do. But no, in this section I really needed you to identify your strengths. This is where even the most academic of people usually stutter or get lost with their reply. This is because we are not used to saying what our strengths are, what we are good at. But, believe me, you need to *believe* that you have got something to offer, something to shout about.

SO THAT WASN'T SO HARD WAS IT?

Whenever I speak about affirmations I do feel that I should be holding my hands in the air and singing as I speak them. But, they have changed the way in which I think and in the way I allow others to make me think. You and only you are in control of your thoughts!

HOW TO BRING DOWN THE WHOLE DEPARTMENT OR WORKFORCE

Why do you think it is important that an employer see's that you have a positive attitude?

Because if not, you are more likely to bring a work place or department down. Again, this is not just from what employers think, but from personal experience too.

Did you know it can take just *one* persons' attitude to demoralise the workforce? And this has been from *professionals.* Verging on the side of *bullying.* Believe me it's true, so an employer, regardless of what qualifications you have, if you come across as *negative not a people person,* even if you have every qualification going then they are less likely to hire you.

Remember I have been in the position of almost every example I have given you. And this one really does make me want to swear. I know if I was the employer, I would be looking at your personal skills more closely than you think.

NEGATIVITY BREEDS NEGATIVITY

Have a think with your own experience; have you come across somebody who has had such a negative attitude that you felt drained? It could be in the pub, at school, college, workplace or anywhere. So try and come across with a positive attitude.

Like I say to the learners, I realise that you cannot always have a positive attitude, we all have our own personal life, our own personal problems. But, as I mentioned in the *work ethic* section, you need to overcome this for the time in which you are at work.

Again, speaking from experience I have gone through quite a lot of things, but I still got up, went to work and carried out my job to the very best of my ability. Even when I could barley lift my head up, even when I had gone through some horrible moments.

In situations like this there could be times when you need to wear a *mask*. Yes, I have heard the jokes, *"Tracey, you're still wearing yours."* But joking aside, there are times when you need to cover up your emotions with a mask (obviously not a real mask)!

Remember, you could still be on probation; you may want to move up and progress within the company. By keeping a positive outlook, you are far more likely to succeed.

WHY DO YOU DESERVE A JOB?

So what do you know about self belief, esteem and confidence? Ask yourself this question and tell yourself how good you are. I am going to ask a couple of questions either write them down or say them out loud (or in your head if you prefer). Imagine I am asking these questions in an aggressive manner. Sock it to me and give me dam good reasons.

Why should you be given the chance of employment?

_____

_____

_____

Why do you deserve a promotion?

_____

_____

_____

Who do you think you are, wanting to change your career?

_____

_____

_____

Hopefully you have really laid it on why you should get employed, promotion or change careers. Don't let anyone tell you differently, you can do it. I know. I have been there. I learnt to tell my nagging second voice (in our head) to do one. Otherwise, we will do what this second voice is saying and it's not always right. We will lose the chance to experience opportunities.

CREATE YOUR OWN LADDER OF LIFE

Hopefully by now you will have become more confident that you do deserve that job or promotion. If you have struggled with this part then re-do the exercises until you firmly believe that you are just as good as the next person. What I want you to do now is to create your own 'ladder of life', create your own goals. After all, we all need to have an aim in life, something to focus on no matter how big or small.

So have a look at the following:

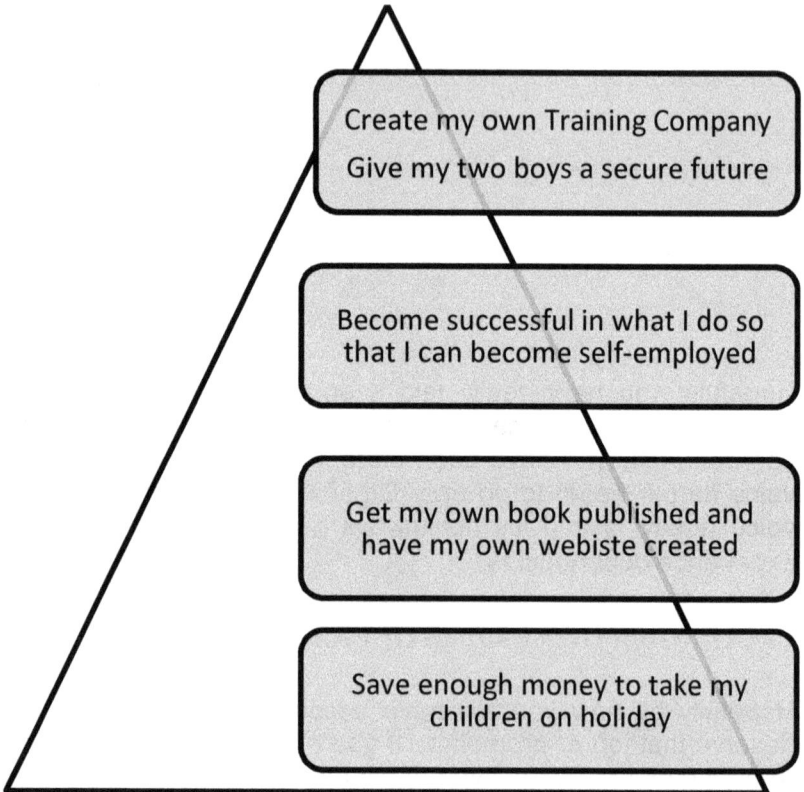

```
        ╱╲
   ┌────────────────────────────┐
   │ Create my own Training Company │
   │ Give my two boys a secure future │
   └────────────────────────────┘
     ┌────────────────────────────┐
     │ Become successful in what I do so │
     │  that I can become self-employed  │
     └────────────────────────────┘
       ┌──────────────────────────┐
       │ Get my own book published and │
       │  have my own webiste created  │
       └──────────────────────────┘
         ┌────────────────────────┐
         │ Save enough money to take my │
         │      children on holiday      │
         └────────────────────────┘
```

I am being really honest here when I say this took me ages to think about my own aims and goals. To me each one is a massive step to reach, but I will reach it, maybe not this year or the next but I will at some point in my life. But it is also important to remember that you can change your goals, you may go down another path (career change etc). But you need an aim as this will give you the motivation and determination to succeed.

156

EXAMPLE OF HOW TO REACH GOALS

Firstly I need to make sure I have full time employment to pay for the basic needs (mortgage, bills, food, phone, children etc). Then with each small amount I have saved I would like to think that I could afford to take the children away for at least a week's holiday within the next two years.

Next, I need to believe in myself that I can continue with this book, (if you're reading this then crikey I have done it). Then I need to understand how and/or who could help me create a website, maybe I need to go to college etc for this. Who will run the website? I will still need to be working full time to pay for the bills.

My ultimate goal at the top would to be self-employed. I would love to give talks around the country on 'how to become employable', or 'how to secure that promotion'. I would love to go to different parts of the sector which is involved within employability and tell them how I think we should address un-employment issues.

And do you know, I am scared of all of the above. Somebody like me doesn't have ideas above their station, because these are all above what I have ever done before.

So what's the point in carrying on with my aims and goals? Well for one thing, I actually believe that I can do it because of my passion for teaching and educating others. And the other reason is that I have finally found self-belief. Now many people who know me will say that I had lots of this anyway, but for the people who really do know me then they will know that I have faced many struggles and situations and I have lacked this wonderful skill – having self-belief, believing that I am worthy of good things.

157

Believing that I have an enormous amount of empathy and understanding of situations to make a difference to peoples' lives. Bloody hell, I am almost crying here, do you know why? This is the first time I have actually come out and said all that, so again I am continually pushing myself through my own barriers.

CREATING YOUR OWN LADDER OF LIFE

I want you to take a look at what you want to achieve in the next few years. Don't be scared to put the manager or team leader because you can achieve anything you set your mind to.

I have added two diagrams in case you are torn between your goals and aims. You can add more if you wish, I just added four sections for you to get you started. One thing I must say is that the goals you set must be realistic and something you can feel is not out of your reach. You may need to break the goals down even further; for example to get a job you first need to look at what you have to offer and what you would like to do. Then use all of the tips in this book.

Once you have created the perfect C.V(s) you need to remain positive that a job is out there for you! If you really want that job or promotion, you will get it. Just keep believing.

Create your own ladder, state what you want and aim for it.

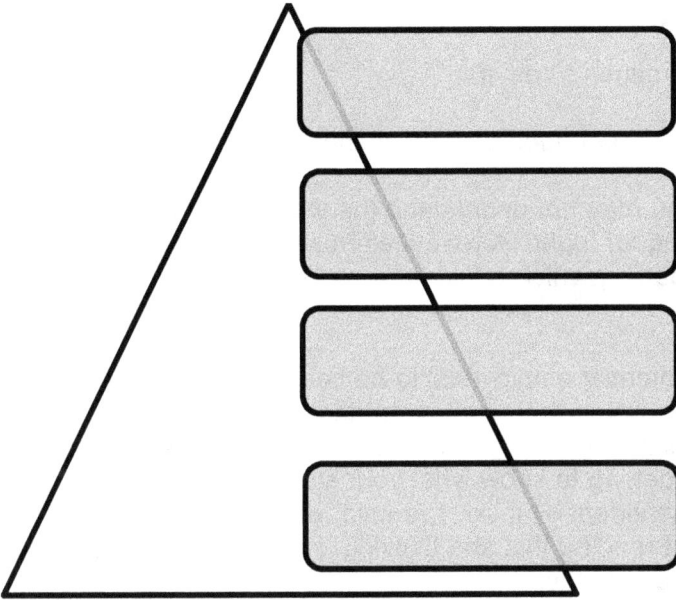

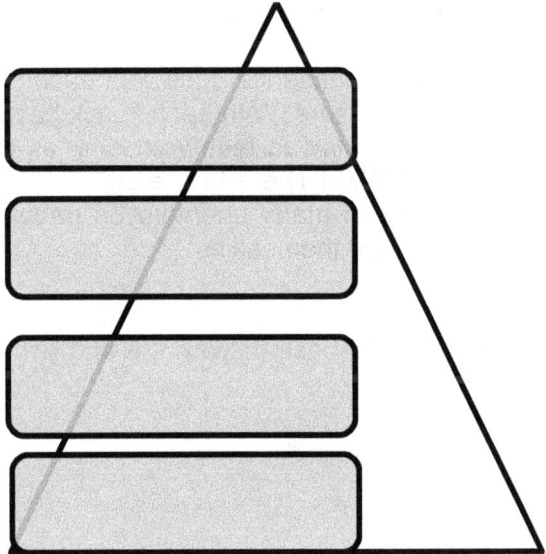

159

RE-CAP AND CONSOLIDATION

So, what is an affirmation? Yes, it's:

"It's one of them reet good sentences that sounds dead nice."

I do realise that you may not understand the word 'reet', apologies. It's just Yorkshire twang for 'right'. Anyway, affirmations are sentences that have a deeper meaning which could help you to train your thoughts to be positive.

Employers want potential employees' to be confident in themselves, to be able to be confident in their own strengths and abilities. They want to see that you believe in yourself. Okay, you may not be I know that. With practice and getting to know what your strengths are you will start to become more confident. But like I've said, you need to put the work in. It's no good just reading this and thinking 'yeah' 'yeah'. Tell yourself how good you are every day.

For those of you who are un-employed, you need to practice this more and really shout out how good you are. I feel, with speaking to my learners' that confidence goes with each rejection letter. With each trip to see their advisors. With each knock back.
Many (not all) start to feel worthless, as though they have nothing to offer. YOU HAVE! There I have shouted at you because I truly see the determination of many unemployed people who are just waiting for a chance to prove themselves.

I know that to believe in yourself is hard, really I do. But get that positive attitude back in your life and you will see how things start to look up.

THE ROSE THAT DIES OR THE PLASTIC ROSE THAT LIVES

Somebody once told me that one way to look at our confidence and self-belief is to imagine that you are a flower (please bare with me here), you flourish in the sun, you experience different days: hot, warm, bees, being watered, being fed, gaining something new each day and being admired and watched by many. Then the seasons start to change, you start to lose your petals. You're starting to die. Come a few months time you will be no more.

Now imagine that you're the plastic rose. You are stood there shining, a glossy coat of colours, never going to die. You can keep going for years and years.

What does this mean? How does this link to employability? Which would you be?

This links because many of us stay in the comfort zone I mentioned earlier on. We are quite happy to be the plastic rose; no harm is going to come to us.

But look at the rose that dies. Look at the opportunity it has gone through. Each day is new and brings something different. Yes it is going to die, but bloody hell they are taking each opportunity that comes along before they do.

YOUR PERSONAL NOTE PAGE

In the space below, write down any thoughts, ideas and notes you feel
will help you throughout the book.

_____

_____

_____

_____

_____

_____

_____

_____

_____

_____

_____

_____

_____

_____

_____

_____

_____

STEP 7

FIRST IMPRESSIONS COUNT

AIM:	Make a fantastic first impression and realise when this impression starts.
OBJECTIVES:	By the end of this session you will be able to:

    ✓ State the importance of first impressions.

    ✓ Develop the impression you will be giving.

    ✓ Explain when you will be first judged on your first impression.

    ✓ List first impressions which could be vital at your interview.

    ✓ Become self aware.

When do you think that you're making an impression? Do you think that first impressions start when you are meeting your prospective employer or interviewer?

Within this section, I promise I am not trying to teach you how to 'suck eggs' or to patronise you in any way. But first impressions need to be taken into consideration; there is a really important message in this session.

You're Being Judged – Come On Down

How many seconds does it take for somebody to start judging you on your first impressions?

Roughly, in about seven seconds you are been visually judged by the interviewer.

Many are already placing you in the position you have applied for to see how you *fit in*.

FIRST IMPRESSIONS THAT YOU DIDN'T REALISE

Okay, how do you make a fantastic first impression? Many people will say that you need to wear a nice suit. Yep, that's right. But the list is more intense than that. When do you think you are being judged on first impressions? Again, most people will say when they are sat in the interview room with the interviewers. Wrong!

The minute you arrive at the job interview, pull up in the car park, get off the bus and even walk down the road, this is when you could be judged. Let me give you one of my own examples from my own experience:

Going to an interview I was almost 1 hour too early so I decided to wait in a coffee shop nearby. As I was queuing at the counter a lady stood at my side, she pushed in. Now, being the typical loudmouth that I am I would normally have said something. But on this particular incident I didn't (maybe my nerves got the better of me). Anyway, it was time to go for the interview. Guess who I saw first, yes the lady who had just pushed in front of me in the coffee shop. She worked on reception, I smiled politely thinking; *"Thank bloody goodness I kept my mouth shut."*

So anyway, back to first impressions. Never under-estimate the importance of sending out positive first impressions. Let me give you another example of first impressions, this is when I used to interview people within my role of retail manager:

I had around five people to see in one day, out of these five people, three really impressed me. I decided to phone these people to ask them to call back in for a second interview the next day. Dinner time came and I decided to nip in to the nearby supermarket, now extreme or unlucky as it is, I overheard a conversation (yes, I was being nosey).

165

But one of the candidates I had called back for a second interview was also in the supermarket telling her friend that she had a second interview. Then what she went on to say is:

"It's a job; I even said that I have often shopped there. I wouldn't buy their crap."

Guess how many people were still in the running for the job? Two, yes. I did still interview the women, but I asked her about our products and the value we offer customers. Straight away I could see from how she spoke and her facial expressions that she was not going to support the company. Oh, and the fact it also told me that she was lying through her teeth.

I really need to give you one more important example which happened recently. A learner had an interview (he had just finished learning the skills which you are learning now), he came back to feedback to me. He said that the first impression he made was with the Security Guard, the learner was quite nervous so he had started talking to him. After his interview, the security guard said; *"I think you would do okay here mate, you are very polite and easy going. It's my mate who's interviewed you so I am going to mention how approachable and friendly you are."*

This learner had not had an interview for 2 years and was scarred by the last one, he said that he took on board everything that I had said and felt that he could go for any job. Result.

Again, you may think this is extreme, but it happens. So get into your mind that the first impression will start the minute you leave the house and you can let your guard down only when you return home.

166

So I have given you examples on first impressions, I want you to make a list of what you feel you would need to take into account when making a fantastic first impression. What do you wear? What do you not do?

As mentioned earlier, I don't want to patronise anyone. But from my experience when teaching this session I always give knowledge and information that the learner didn't even take into account. So have a think about how you are going to make sure that your first impression will have a *positive impact* on the interviewer.

On the next page I will tell you what I have looked for in my role as an interviewer, I bet you will be surprised at what other things you need to take into account.

Create your first impressions list here:

1.
2.
3.
4.
5.
6.
7.
8.

You may have identified more than eight, if so great (smart arse).

You will probably have got some, if not most of what I am going to say on the next page. But I am now in my role of interviewer; take a look at what I would be looking out for.

10 In-Depth Ways To Make Your Mark

But I am now going to take this further, I am going to list a few examples but I will expand on them. This is where you need to be *self-aware*:

FIRST IMPRESSION	THE IMPACT or OUTCOME
1. Interview outfit	Smart, clean, ironed, fresh (smell them as sometimes they can smell like wet dog as they have not been used often). **Ladies**, sorry, but look at your interview shirt or blouse and check to see if it is gaping around the breast area. If so either buy a bigger size or put a vest underneath and leave it open. Make sure you don't have any ladders in your tights. Men and women should check their shoes, do they need a clean? **Men**, sorry but in my experience it is the men I need to say this to, if you are wearing trainers (hopefully not) for heaven's sake clean them and smell them. I have been gipping (retching) at the smell in class at the stench that can seep from footwear.
2. Get a wash	Again, sorry. But people don't always realise that they smell. What I say to my learners' is to go home and smell the armpits of their clothes (usually because the smell is overpowering in class). Also your hair can smell (especially if you've been cooking), if not washed regularly so get it washed.

168

FIRST IMPRESSION	THE IMPACT or OUTCOME
3. Shave	Aimed at the men really (okay, we all know a female who this could apply to), designer stubble is okay, but if it is messy and resembles a massive fur ball on your face then trim it back.
4. Piercings	Many people have piercings and it is part of their image, I understand that. But, some employers will **judge** you on your piercings (wrongly I know). So take them out, secure your job, and then put them back in. Right this bit is mainly for the **ladies** as it is them that I mainly need to have a word with: **tongue piercings**, take it out. I can almost guarantee that if not you will be playing with it, rolling your tongue around it, bringing it onto your lips. Yes, you all agree I bet. So for the duration of the interview I advise you to leave the piercings at home.
5. Tattoo's	Now I personally love some tattoos and I know that many have them done because they mean something to the individual. So all I will say on this matter is have a think, do you need to wear a long sleeve shirt to cover them? Remember, I understand that a tattoo is part of a persons' identity (I too have a lovely one), but sometimes we may need to cover it up for the duration of the interview.

Phew, hope you have taken something from the above list. I have not finished yet, I am going to give you another example.

169

This time it is about the **interview outfit**. Listen, I know that for some people, money may be tight, but really have a think about your outfit.

This next example is from a lovely lady who I had the pleasure to teach:

*I asked everyone to attend the session in their interview outfit. Exactly as they would if they where to go for a proper interview. This lady in particular had a pair of white tracksuit bottoms on (they did look like trousers from afar). I asked her to turn around so that I could look at her backside, **black** underwear on. She informed me that she didn't own any white underwear. She didn't think you could see through them. So I asked her see if she had any black trousers, she had, but again, these were jogging bottoms. I knew that my own trousers and clothes would not fit her so that was out of the question. So she had to make do with the black jogging bottoms (again, they did look like trousers from a distance). But at least we couldn't see her knickers.*

This is where we need to be *self-critical*, look at ourselves; would **you** hire **you** if you were an employer?

Ask somebody who you trust to give you advice on your appearance. It's not that we are scruffs; it can be just that we don't often pay that much attention to ourselves.

FIRST IMPRESSION	THE IMPACT or OUTCOME
6. Deodorant/aftershave/perfume	Lack of it, or too blooming much. Again, remember this is all from experience of what I have had to say to my learners. So obviously, use deodorant but don't use it to mask underlying smells. But also don't go overboard with it either; you don't want your interviewer choking? The same applies to the ladies, but in this case please don't go to the interview smelling like a walking advert for a perfume chain.
7. Smile	A lot of people take this for granted. Let me tell you, watch how you smile, if you go in there smiling as though you have just won the lottery then I am sure the interviewer or indeed any of the employee's could assume that your high on drugs or high on medication! Smiling is important, but don't overdo it. Look at yourself in the mirror – go on do it now. Okay how did you look? A simple smile not a full up curled mouth smile.

Even though these things may be obvious to many of us, they are also the things that we take for granted. Therefore we become too complacent, we think we know all of this as it is common sense. But, quite often we forget to carry out these checks. Almost done with our first impression session, but just a few more first impressions I want you to take on board.

171

FIRST IMPRESSION	THE IMPACT or OUTCOME
8. Personal style	By this, look at your hair. Is it a throw back from the 70's? Have you got a Mohican? Or just some plain 'dodgy hair do'. Again, I am not trying to tell you to lose your identity, but I am afraid if you want to be considered as a likely (and likeable) candidate then look closely to what you look like. It's okay to have your personal style of clothes that separates you from the 'norm', but again just think about how you would judge somebody if you were the interviewer.
9. Walking	Do you have a 'swagger'? Do you normally walk with your hands inside your pockets with a 'don't care' attitude (even if you really do care)? Are you so laid back and overly confident when you walk? Do you walk with your head down to avoid eye contact? Think about this, again it comes down to what the interviewers' perception of you is.
10. Eye Contact	Again, get this right. We all know the importance of good eye contact, but do you know you can over do it. Naturally look around, don't move your head to do this just avert your eyes. One tip is to gently lower your eyes to the tip of the interviewers' nose. Don't stare all the way through. Just imagine if you stared all the way through, and had a big cheesy grin on your face too. Not only would you put your prospective employer off, but you could end up being escorted of the premises for being a 'bit weird'. Okay, that last bit won't happen it's just an image that came into my mind.

I have left these two until the last. After I have given the tips to you I will then give you a couple of examples of where I have experienced this. Remember, I will never teach you anything which I fully don't believe in myself. Everything I am saying to you has happened; therefore I want you to benefit from other people's mistakes.

Now, before I give you the last two, take a look at your hands and feet. Go on, inspect them further. What do they look like? I may come across as a sexist here but here goes. You ladies, look closely at your hands/feet, every part. What do you see? Gents, you do the same. These first impressions usually get forgotten about.

FIRST IMPRESSION	THE IMPACT or OUTCOME
11. Your hands and feet	At this point I will get the learners to look at their hands and then hold them out for me to take a closer look. This is what I usually find: • Chipped nail polish • Dirty nails • Nicotine stains • Dirty ground in muck • False nails with a couple missing I also mentioned feet, if it was a warm summers' day, then usually and acceptably a women may wear open toed shoes. Please, be aware of your feet in the same way as your hands. I mentioned that women may wear opened toed shoes; I aimed this at the women as I would not expect a man to do the same. Again, you may think I am being picky. But the whole point of this book is to give you every bit of knowledge I have passed onto my learners, this has then played some part in securing that *job* or that *promotion*.

173

12. Your handshake	Practice your hand shake; do you know you can tell a lot about a person by their hand shake? Too weak and you come across as unconfident, shy, not up to the challenge of the job. Too firm and you can come across as cocky, arrogant and hard to work with. Again, these are simple steps you can develop, shake hands with your partner to practice.

THE JOB ROLE AND FIRST IMPRESSIONS

What type of job have you applied for? What are they looking for? Is it in retail fashion? Typically, every job role will be advertised with what the employer or company is looking for. For instance, retail you will be advertising the company each day you are there. So you are probably going to be the first person a potential customer will have contact with. How many times have you looked at a sales assistant and thought; *"What **are** they wearing?"* or *"Well they look fed up, I am glad I'm not working here."* Or any other thought, and it is these thoughts that could make your customers go somewhere else. So an employer will not take that chance.

The next time you're out and about shopping, have a look around you. Are the sales assistants or checkout operators cheery and smiley? Or have you experienced any negative first impressions? I certainly know I have. I shall not give you an example of this; I may need to shop there again!

So just take a look, even when you're phoning a company or a company is phoning you. We still make first impressions even if it isn't face to face.

One of my learners wanted to go back into retail (at a jewellers shop) the first thing I looked at and noticed was the chipped nail polish and her mucky finger nails. Not a good look regardless of which job you were going for.

174

My own first impression was (putting it politely) *"What a scruff, they're not bothered about themselves."* So, why should an employer be bothered about them?

WHAT NOT TO DO REGARDING FIRST IMPRESSIONS

You may think this is obvious, but again as mentioned earlier I am planting a seed inside your mind. Just make sure you exercise this seed and practice the skills learnt. We often *miss* the important things because we are so used to doing them.

So what do you think you shouldn't do which could give bad first impressions? Have a think and list below:

1.
2.
3.
4.

This list is not as intense as the previous but I want to go through it so you are harmed with every bit of knowledge.

Did you think of any? On the next page I have just given a few tips.

175

So you are raring to go for those all important interviews. So don't go and blow it by doing the following:

WHAT NOT TO DO	IMPACT- OUTCOME
1. Turn up late	I bet you're saying to yourself *"this is a waste of time, I know this."* Good, I am glad you know this but let me tell you I have experienced this with my learners and from previous roles so many times. Make sure you are prepared for any eventuality, Buses running late, Train strikes/not running.
2. Smell of booze	You may be shaking your head at this point, but I can honestly tell you this happens. I won't give you an example (she will guess it is her) but even if you went out the night before, you can still reek of stale alcohol.
3.Smell of smoke/weed	I know you will be nervous, try and not have a cigarette until after the interview. Or if you do, make sure you wash your hands and have a mint. I mention weed here, all too often people don't realise how strong this smell can be, and more importantly how everyone will know you've been smoking it. Straight away a big fat cross will be at the side of your name in the interview.
4. Watch what you eat	Garlic and spicy foods which gives off a strong smell should be avoided at least 2 days before your interview. Make sure you have brushed your teeth before the interview; I know I am just saying that's all. You don't want to be sat there singing your own praises and you have a piece of lettuce or yesterday's dinner still in your teeth on show do you!
5. Chew gum	Please take your chewing gum out and get rid of it before your interview. They don't want to see you chewing away!

Another example I want to share is when I was explaining about first impressions. One man in particular informed the whole group that, *"You must have met our lass."* When I asked what he meant he reeled off the following:

- She stinks
- She doesn't brush her teeth
- She has hairy armpits
- She doesn't realise how bad she can smell

Obviously I didn't laugh at this point (of course I did), I asked the person if he had ever sat her down and pointed these things out to her. Or if anyone had. His reply was, *"No, she would kick off and say I was being nasty to her."*

And that could be the point sometimes, we just don't like saying to somebody that they smell. So, put down the book, and have a smell of your armpits. I am actually being serious, get a T-Shirt or your coat and smell the armpits on that. If it smells then wash it. I know I have gone overboard maybe on all of the first impressions but remember this:

I speak from actual experience of others doing many of the above. I know many of you think that it is just *'common sense'*, and I do agree with you. But like I have already said, sometimes we get too complacent and laid back or worry too much about the interview, that we forget the importance of *first impressions*.

RE-CAP AND CONSOLIDATION

As you can see, first impressions go further than you may have thought. I always say to the learners' that even though we are not supposed to judge people, quite often we do. Think about it, when did you last look at somebody and 'slag' them off, either to your friend/partner etc or just in your own mind?

Well if you can sit there, hand on heart say that you have never had any negative thoughts about another person – well good on you. I know I certainly have made judgement on a first impression. Believe me; future employers would also make the same judgement too.

So in short, be prepared and arrive on time. Turn up looking smartly groomed, dressed and make sure your hair is not greasy. Use sufficient deodorant and perfume but don't overdo it.

If you need to smoke, make sure you clean your hands and have a mint or three before the interview. Don't have alcohol the night before, and certainly don't sit in a pub having a sneaky drink just before your interview.

You can tell a lot from a persons' footwear, make sure they are clean and stink free!

Okay, I don't need to go on anymore I hope you get the message. If not, re-read this section again.

YOUR PERSONAL NOTE PAGE

In the space below, write down any thoughts, ideas and notes you feel
will help you throughout the book.

_____

_____

_____

_____

_____

_____

_____

_____

_____

_____

_____

_____

_____

_____

_____

_____

_____

_____

_____

179

STEP 8

APPLICATION FORMS

AIM:	To get it right the first time and create that great first impression.
OBJECTIVES:	By the end of this session you will be able to:

      ✓ Start off your first impression.

      ✓ Explain why a company would want an application form instead of your C.V.

      ✓ Recognise a key feature within your application form.

Within this section I want to highlight some common mistakes I have seen over the years. Remember, your application form is your first impression. Don't mess it up.

Again, you may not think you will bother with this section but I am going to tell you about one important part on the form. Yes, other information is important but many of you often leave out a vital piece of information.

I will hold up my hands and say that I have messed up application forms before and I have only noticed when I have uploaded it to the website and sent it. Needless to say I didn't hear from this particular company. Each company may have their own application forms; others will just accept your C.V and cover letter. Many of my learners will bring in their application forms for me to look over.

10 COMMON MISTAKES FOUND ON APPLICATION FORMS

Usually I see many mistakes like the following on an application form; you cannot afford even one tiny error on it.

Problem	What the interviewer/recruiter will think
Not following instructions	Like a *bull in a China shop*, that's what we are at times. We don't spend two minutes reading the instructions first. We just plough straight in and often make mistakes.
Proof reading errors	Within my years in education, proof – reading was something I was known for banging on about. The learners used to love it if I made a mistake (I hated it!). You must proof read your work and even ask somebody else to look through it, a fresh pair of eyes can make all the difference and more than likely they will spot a mistake.
Crossing out details incorrectly	Sometimes you may be asked to cross out the relevant option (yes/no), when actually you meant the opposite.

	You are saying that you don't take care when carrying out a task, you are careless and don't think important things through.
Mistakes in the form, especially your own address	This is a typical example: 12 Cedar ~~Road,~~ Avenue, Carleton Glen, Wf6 5gG Believe me this is a very common mistake to make, and you need to remember that a postcode is always in capital letters. This again tells the interviewer that you are not organised (otherwise you would have wrote this out in rough first), no attention to detail.
Employment history too long	Usually there is not a lot of space to write down your employment history, so I would recommend you write down your most recent and practice this by writing it out in rough first; you will be able to correctly transfer all relevant details. So that the interviewer/recruiter doesn't think any negative thoughts about you, you could always add another sheet of paper to the form. I would still recommend you try and get it all down though.
Smudge marks from the pen or grease from the fingers	Individual is not bothered about appearance and they are not bothered about making a good impression. Not bothered or motivated in general.

I have almost done with the application form. So far what do you think?
Have you made any of the errors I have mentioned?
These are really all too common faults and mistakes; take a look at the next page.

This is where we *waffle* on and forget the point of the application form. An employer is wanting to know what they are going to get out of you.

Problem	What the interviewer/recruiter will think
Your school and/or college qualifications are too long	To keep your form looking smart and professional the last thing you want is to overload it. Again, do a rough copy first and then practice putting it all down. What you could do if you have a lot of qualifications is again, write them all down in full and attach the sheet of paper to the form. This must be done is a professional and accurate manner.
Work experience/voluntary work	If you cannot think of something and your fresh out of college or school then put down your *work experience* which you will have gone on from the school. This would normally be for two weeks so really try and think about what you did. If you left it blank the interviewer/recruiter could think that there may be a reason why nobody has allowed you to work at their company for experience.
Health/disabilities	On some application forms they could be a section on health/disabilities. You must tell them if you have either, but what a lot of people do is they say they have this wrong and that wrong. When in actual fact they have not being diagnosed they are just assuming. Will an interviewer/recruiter think that you are a hypochondriac?

Your qualifications gained at school? A tough one especially if you have none; like me. So what do I do? I leave this out and make sure I have every other qualification on that I have gained.

184

If you're running short on space then you may have to leave something out. Again, like your C.V, they don't really care what you did 20 years ago.

NOW FOR THE BIG ONE

I have left this out on purpose as I feel that many people don't understand the value of the next box:

> **Any other additional information to support your application form to be written down here:**

Have a think. What would you put down here? Quite often this page could be as long as an A4 sheet of paper, which we still leave out. You could also be asked to use another blank sheet of paper to add to the application form.

A Vital Selling Point We Usually Miss Out

If you put down 'No' or leave it blank then shame on you. This is your chance to bang it to them. Tell them what you're about, how you can add value, how you have the necessary skills for the job, and how passionate, caring, enthusiastic, motivated and loyal person you are. This is your last time to shine; you last time to sell yourself.

Okay I don't expect you to put all of that down. But here is another secret to gaining that interview; never leave this box blank, look at the job description and tailor to suit you and what you can bring to the company (similar to how I have told you to tailor your C.V and cover/spec letters).

Look at the job advert below:

Shop 'til' U Drop – Sales Assistant

Experienced and flexible individual required. Excellent communication skills and a passion for people are essential to this job role. An outgoing personality who displays enthusiasm and motivation are essential to this job role.

Please send your application form to Mr D Sachs, Job Ref: 092929

So, let us just pretend that we have only one part left to fill in, this is how I would recommend you do it:

Any other additional information to support your application form to be written down here:

With an outgoing and charismatic personality I have a real passion for people and understand how important effective customer care is. I have had 2 years experience in this field and due to my flexible and adaptable nature I have helped to increase sales, as I feel that by going above and beyond for the customer and company is an essential part of the work. I am motivated and enthusiastic to learn new skills and will always be willing to support my colleagues throughout any challenges we may face. With excellent communication skills I quickly build a rapport with customers and colleagues.

Can you see how useful this box is? So look at the job description and tailor it to suit you. Obviously if you haven't had 2 years experience then don't put that. You cannot lie; you just are selling your skills. This will then take you a step further to an interview.

Again, you need to be the person who you are describing, but more importantly, you need to be able to 'back it up', (I will go through this more later) with situations, tasks, actions and results.

You need to be aware of each step of the employment process.

RECAP AND CONSOLIDATION

What's the main thing you must realise about your application form? That it is your first impression. If you have applied for job after job using application forms and/or by sending your C.V and you are not even getting a sniff of an interview then something is wrong.

There is a reason why this is happening. So your application form needs to be spot on. Not one mistake, no tippex to be used. It needs to be perfect. But I will say this again, if you have not heard from any of the companies who you are sending your application form or C.V to then become *self aware*, be honest with yourself. Are you selling yourself short? Are you rushing the form? Have you manipulated your C.V to fit to the job being advertised?

Get somebody to proof read your work. Honestly, spend a few extra minutes on your form and/or C.V and get someone else's opinion. When completing application forms, have your C.V at the side of you to take down specific information.

Again, by researching the company first, you can look at their *aims, values and goals* etc and add these to the '*additional information*' part. It's all about standing out from the crowd and getting the employer to like you, so that you can get a foot in the door for an interview.

YOUR PERSONAL NOTE PAGE

In the space below, write down any thoughts, ideas and notes you feel will help you throughout the book.

STEP 9

COMMUNICATION

AIM:	Communicate effectively at various levels and explain the 'pie' chart of communication.
OBJECTIVES:	By the end of this session you will be able to: ✓ Recognise what communication is. ✓ Develop awareness of body language. ✓ State why communication is important. ✓ Explain why employers' value communication skills. ✓ Recognise how communication can be broken down.

191

Never underestimate the importance of this section. Within my sessions I always inform the learners that communication is not a standalone section. Communication will have been embedded throughout everything they have done on the course.

This is where I really need you guys to really *take ownership* of your learning. Obviously, it would be easier if you were in class with me so that we can develop this very important skill. So we will do the next best thing.

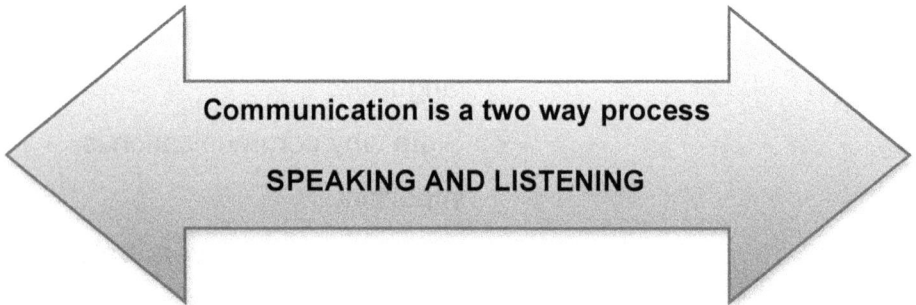

Communication is a two way process

SPEAKING AND LISTENING

IF YOU WANT A JOB, THEN READ THIS

The first thing I want you to do is think about body language. We have all heard about it, well now you are going to learn even more. Below is a 'pie chart' of body language and I want you to either mentally place the words given or actually write it on the chart (maybe not, in case you get it wrong).

You can see that the chart is split into three sections; where would you place each of the communication key words?

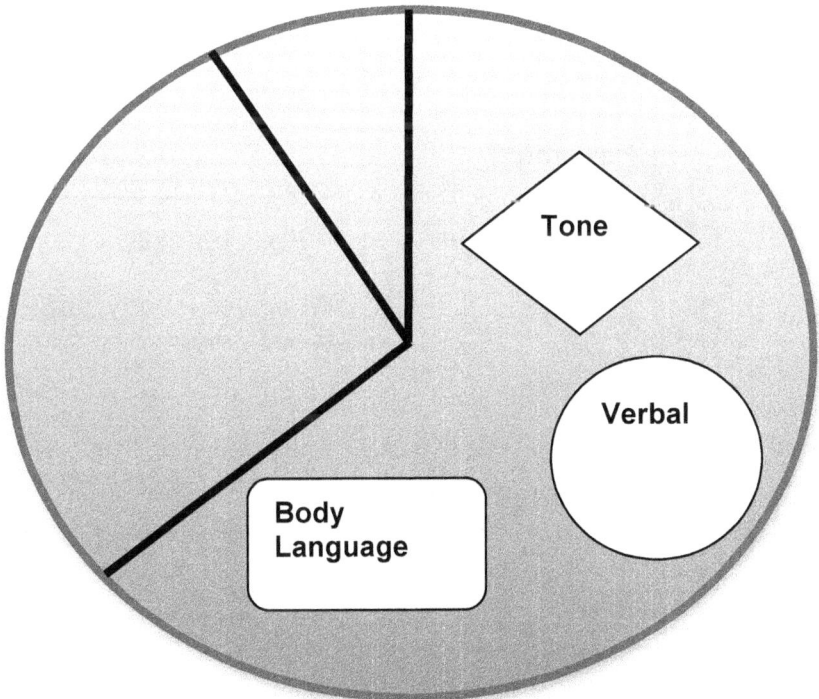

193

How did you do? Well I am hoping I am shocking you here (and hoping that you didn't take a sneaky peek). I can honestly say that when I researched this I was wrong with my initial choices. And many of my learners are too shocked by the actual answers.

As you can see, body language is one of the main ways in which we communicate. Link that to the first impression section then you will appreciate that some of you may have a lot of work to do.

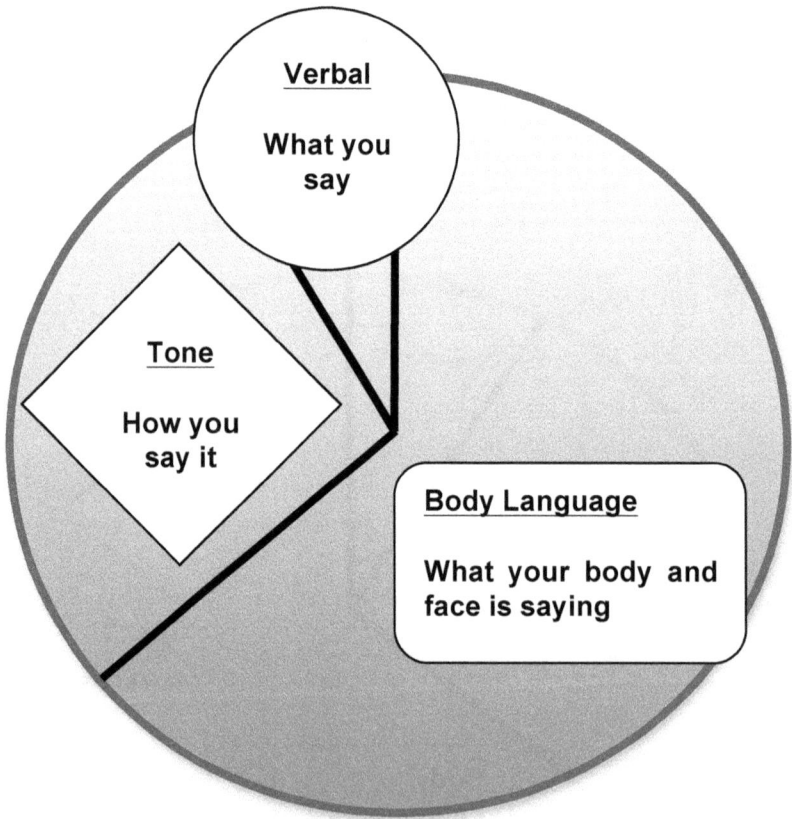

Verbal

What you say

Tone

How you say it

Body Language

What your body and face is saying

194

A BREAK DOWN IN COMMUNICATIONS

Don't worry; we are going to go through some examples. Now for a bit of Math! No, we're not really because I hate it, but I will show you some interesting percentages:

Communication Broken Down

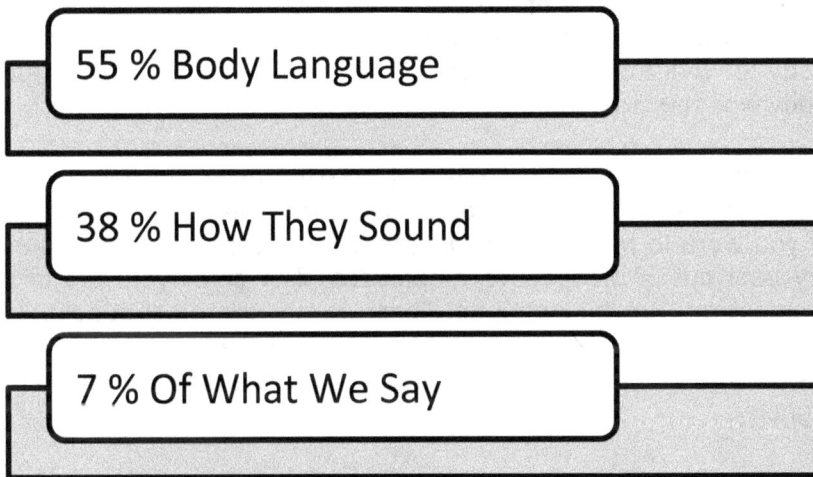

55 % Body Language

38 % How They Sound

7 % Of What We Say

I am going to take you through each of the above stages and explain through examples and experiences on why you need to understand this part of the communication process. Again, I cannot stress enough how important this section is.

Get this wrong, and I can probably lay bets that you will struggle to gain employment or progress within the company.

Why?

195

Because who the hell wants to employ somebody who cannot speak correctly, who won't listen to others and who has a poor *communication technique*? Somebody who constantly looks fed up and bored (even though they may not be).

You will be like too much hard work, so they will go for the one who uses *effective communication* throughout their interview.

BECOME THE EMPLOYER

Put yourself into the shoes of the employer, you own the company and you have £15,000 or even £8,000 (just random figures) to pay somebody to work for you. How do you feel if you are presented with somebody who has poor communication skills?

You know what, forget those figures, it doesn't matter what they are paying or how little it is. The money still comes from the company. Even if you were to be offered *minimum wage*, every employer wants the very best out of prospective employees. The employers are in a fantastic position, just think about it. There are thousands of people out there who are highly skilled, have great life experience and so many qualities to offer and the lucky employer can have a pick out of a very good bunch.

So to the first scenario, what would you do if you were the employer? The key to gaining fantastic *employability skills* is to look at it from the employer or interviewers point of view.

Yes, you would want a fantastic person who had all of the skills we have gone through so far. And what lets you down, the way that you bloody communicate. Normally when teaching I would really lay this down and my learners think I have turned into a character from Jekyll and Hyde. This is because I need to re-enforce the importance of communication skills.

Usually I have numerous activities for the learners to complete. Again, this won't work within the book so I will try and explain through real life experience and examples from my learners and my own experience.

196

Right, let's get down to it! Body language, yes I know you will have heard how important it is but do you? Or is it something you just let go over your head because you have never had to really think about it. I did. I thought, yeah okay body language; arms folded and yawning is not to be done. Forget that, yes it is important but I am going to go further into detail.

BODY LANGUAGE FACTS AND WHAT YOU NEED TO KNOW

Basically, body language is when people use their body or facial expressions without realising it. To communicate a message to another person. Time and time again we are letting people know what is happening in our head and in our thoughts without us realising it.

Remember we are judged by people usually within seven seconds, so if you're waiting for your interview and you are slouched eyes shut (maybe a late night) and constantly yawning. You have already given a message that you're not that interested. A great big fat cross straight away against your name and that's without you even opening your mouth (except to yawn).

Okay let's have a look at another situation; you're sat again in reception, your head is just focused on the floor or on your mobile phone. Can you picture it? How do you think you have come across? Un-approachable and not willing to communicate with others around you? I bet you have *'excellent communicator at all levels'* (or something similar) on your C.V. Then blooming back it up, communication is not just about talking, you need to remember that.

197

Your turn!

Have a think about what other things our body can inform people about without us even realising it. Use the space below if you like to put down your findings:

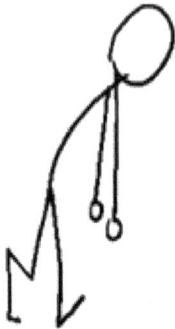

_____

_____

_____

_____

_____

_____

How did you do then? I bet I can expand on those thoughts and ideas you have come up with (unless you're a clever clogs).

198

Below are some of the more common things we do, without realising we are giving off different signals of communication:

- Happiness
- Sadness
- Playing with your hair
- Tilting your head to one side
- Fear, anger, worried
- Confident, surprise
- Don't care, nervous
- Speaking with your hands too close to your mouth
- Bored, arrogant
- Relaxed

I will just say this again, our body language is vital when we meet someone for the first time. Think how you have formed an opinion in the past about somebody within seconds. Well, people are just doing the same thing with you, only your career or success depends on it. Body language can be so influential in forming an impression on someone. Get it right the first time!

To get this point across I would ask learners to take part in an activity, they think I am listening to what they are saying. But to be honest they could be saying; *blah, blah, blah,blah*. I only inform them at the end of the task that I couldn't care less about what they were saying; I only took notice of their body language. And let me tell you, in some cases I fed back to the learners and told them that their body language is telling me a totally different story to what has come out of their mouth.

If you have children, have a think about how many times you have said the following: *"I will know if you're lying."* I have on numerous occasions and I have been right on numerous occasions too (until they grew older and knew how to fool me). That's because we are looking at their body language.

199

Hands up how many of you have been in some sort of meeting or have attended a training course and you were bored to death? Again, I am holding up my hands. I have experienced both and as hard as I try to look interested it is really hard as my subconscious facial features are saying; "*Help, get me out of this place.*" So have a look when you're next out and in contact with others, what body language are they saying to you?

YOUR FACE SAYS A THOUSAND WORDS

Honestly, I cannot stress enough about how we are communicating through body language. A facial expression is one sure way to judge how somebody is feeling. Let me give you an example of this from my own recent experience; my previous boss loved old fashioned programmes and period dramas and decided to inform me on the current events in *Downton Abbey.* I was relatively new to the company so showed interest as he spoke. He then said to me; "*Tracey, am I really boring you?*" I said, "*No, not at all.*" He then replied with, "*Well your face is saying a different thing.*" So being the honest and sometimes outspoken person that I am I had to confess that, "*I would have rather stuck my head in a hot oven than understand what was happening in Downton.*"

Now obviously I said it in a really nice way, well as much as I could. Please don't hold it against me if you are a *Downton* fan, I am sure it is really good but just not my cup of tea!

You could say that I '*wear my heart on my sleeve*', so what I am feeling or thinking quite often is portrayed on my face. This again brings me back to our body language, especially when going for an interview. You may have had a stressful few days with your personal life, and here you are having to sit through an interview with the 'weight of the world' in your mind. Don't muck it up, really try and use the positive thoughts which I covered in an earlier session to get you through the interview.

Don't go explaining the 'why's' on your feelings, they don't care. They just want the best person for the job. Make sure that person is you and leave any dilemmas and problems at home, you can sort them out later.

200

Another test I often use on body language is to have two learner's displaying body language and the other learners have to guess what they are saying. Guess what, not once have the learners all agreed on this. What one person thinks another thinks differently. So why do you think I have told you this? Because we don't all interpret body language the same. And the same will be for your interviewer; they could all too often miss-read the signals you are giving off.

So to recap on this, (I will go in depth into interviews later) become aware of your own body language, ask your partner or somebody to tell you honestly how you come across at times with your body language. Ask them to tell you when you are giving out *bad body language signals*. Don't take it to heart, but you do need to realise how you may come across at times, without even knowing it.

Be confident (not arrogant) and use the tips listed in the first impression section to display fantastic and positive body language.

Examples Of How Body Language Can Affect Your Interview

Like I have said all the way through this book, I will always give you examples from real life experiences. Here I am going to give you examples of how body language has let people down when it comes to the interview:

Example 1:

My client was going to an interview and I actually knew the manager, I did not arrange this interview but I phoned her up for feedback and this is what she said:

> He answered the questions to a high standard he sat in his chair, slouched and slumped. He then sighed and I took it as though he was not dedicated enough to the role, and that he was just seeking employment anywhere. I just got a negative feel about him.

201

When I fed this back to the individual they were surprised. They thought they had taken on board all my advice. He then said, I wonder if it was because I had an argument with my girlfriend. I just told him that it didn't matter, because he had blown it.

Leave your troubles at home.

Example 2:

One of my young female learners had an interview for childcare. My biggest worry was that she would not come across as confident, even though she is a natural with children. The feedback was:

> She was a lovely girl and I could see potential in her, but her confidence let her down. I don't have the time to build up people's confidence and felt as though I would need to *mother* her. The next candidate who came in was full of confidence without being too arrogant. She got the position instead.

Example 3:

One lady who I deemed as *'so employable'* went for a job interview for a sales assistant. As part of her *tracking*, I needed to follow up her interview and had a discussion with the interviewer, feedback was:

> I loved how she could answer each question which I asked her, but one thing which bothered me was that she kept putting her hands to her mouth so I had to keep repeating the question. Even though I liked what she said, I just got a feeling that she would not cope with the pressure we are often under.

BODY LANGUAGE COUNTS FOR MANY PEOPLE NOT SECURING A JOB

So never under-estimate this important form of communication. Remember if you are called for an interview, then you have already got the interviewer and company interested in you. Body language can be used as a tool to filter people; it's not nice to be judged but it will happen. The interviewer will already be making up their mind on whether they *like* or *dislike* a person. This is the filter. If you are labelled under dislike, then it could be that choose how you answer a question; good or excellent, they have still filtered you into these two categories.

So how do you make sure you're filtered under the *likeable* category? You make sure you use *effective body language*. Ask somebody to be honest with you, what are they reading from your body language? In my sessions I always say what signals the learner is sending out, I've never been wrong yet (smart arse I know).

One sure way to see if a person is lying is to look at their mouth, honestly. When I do one to one interviews and ask an awkward question, I look at their mouths. When the interview has ended I then say, "you lied on *'that question'"*, and they say, *"Yes, how do you know?"* I then tell them that I watched their mouth move differently.

So I have gone through the main category of *unspoken communication*. Now I am going to go through the next crucial stage; *how we sound!*

Are you assertive? Are you aggressive assertive (without even realising it)? Being assertive, especially within the process of gaining employment will make you look more confident. But, aggressive assertiveness is often shown without you realising it.

Your face and tone of voice can usually give this away – especially if you feel awkward and uncomfortable within your interview.

203

Is Your Tone Of Voice Letting You Down?

This is really hard to express through words, I usually give impressions to get my point across (and usually look a right tool). Right, now for your next task:

Welcome To The 'Bores' Of The World

Imagine the most boring person you know. We all know somebody that can bore us to death. Think of a situation when you have been in (maybe at the pub, other social event or at work) somebody's' company. There is always somebody who you may want to try and avoid because the *sound* and *tone* of their voice makes you want to scream and shout *'go away'*. Okay, that may be just me! But think about it. Right have you got someone in mind?

Okay, now think about when they are talking to you and telling you a story. You're trying not to yawn, you're trying to look interested, but your face could be saying a whole different thing. You are not even listening to what they are saying because you *'turned off'* the minute they opened their mouth. Now, the way in which they speak; at one level is their *tone* of voice. In some ways it's like a robot with no feeling or emotion. Even if the story is really interesting, they are boring the living daylights out of you.

The impact is that you lose interest and you don't actually care about their interesting story anymore. Well let me give you some advice (more covered in our interview session), if you want a job, if you want to get promotion then you need to make sure your own voice is not like the one described. This is where you need to be self-aware, be aware of how you really come across.

This is hard; ask somebody how your tone of voice is. Don't take it personally if they say you are boring, accept what they have said and work on it. Practice speaking with more emotion, with more enthusiasm.

Think about your impending interview, they like you because you have made a fantastic first impression with your C.V or application form. Now put yourself into the shoes of your interviewer. They have looked at your C.V and read that you are an 'excellent communicator and can communicate at different levels', and you are an 'enthusiastic individual' (or something similar), you're exactly what they are looking for. But then you open your mouth to answer a question and within around 3 seconds they are thinking, "What the hell," harsh but true.

PRACTICE WHAT YOU PREACH

This links us back to your C.V, can you remember when I said you need to be able to back everything up on your C.V? Well this is where you 'practice what you preach', you become your C.V. You become that passionate and enthusiastic person.

Do you get where I am coming from? Well I am just going to give you a few more examples of the importance of the *tone* of voice you use. Imagine the 'Marks and Spencer' adverts, you know the one; where the woman is selling their products by the tone of her voice. She sounds amazing and gets us interested in what she is saying.

I have never done my food shopping there, but I certainly tried it because the way in which she sounded made it so appealing. At the moment it is a man who has taken over, again, he makes it so appealing by the *enthusiasm* in his voice. This is the *tone*. This is something that you need to practice, especially if you normally come across with no personality or enthusiasm in your voice. Again, don't take it personally; this is another way in which the interviewer will *filter* you and mentally be putting a cross against you.

So let me give you some examples of my experience with tone of voice whilst I was attending a recruitment event.

One man in particular was into I.T and I was very excited to meet him due to our staff shortage. I asked him about his passion for the learner and helping others.

The minute he started talking I thought to myself,' "There is no way on earth this man has any sort of passion or enthusiasm."

Straight away I had filtered him as a 'no way'. You may think that was judgemental and I didn't mean to be, but it is how we are sometimes programmed. Put people into boxes and judge. Now if he had shown even a tiny bit on enthusiasm and passion then we would have brought him in for an interview to chat further.

My next scenario is regarding one of my closest friends. She was going for an interviewer for a fantastic job which she had not done before and she was really nervous. After I had given her a pep talk about enthusiasm and passion (not that she needed it I may say), I asked her how it went.

207

This was her response (in short):

> "I can't believe it; they phoned me an hour after and offered me the job. They said that they realise that I will need development, but what they loved was the enthusiasm, drive and passion I showed."

Obviously, being the smart arse I am, I knew they would love her. You just had to talk to her for a few seconds and you could see all that she had to offer an employer.

She backed up everything she had on her C.V. She backed up her claim that she was enthusiastic, passionate and determined.

The interviewers loved her. Even though there were people who had more experience than her, her soft skills and personality shone through.

COME DINE WITH US

Within my sessions I use a resource called *'Come Dine With Us.'* I want you to try it out, I have tailored it to suit this book, but I created it a long time ago and it has been used time and time again in most of the places I have worked to *aid confidence* within communication.

Look at the task and try your best.

Scenario:

You are appearing on 'Mars Bar Radio' to sell your meal to the listeners. Remember, it's through communication especially your tone of voice so you need to be very descriptive.

(This would be really good if a partner or friend supported you and joined in. So get asking!)

Pick one from each of the list below

- *Starters*
- *Main Course*
- *Dessert*
- *Drinks*

Once you have chosen your meals, you will need to describe each one to your friend or partner. You will need to *'SELL'* each of the courses to the listeners; using your fantastic communication and describing skills.

- *You need to make us hungry with your words.*
- *Describe the food fully.*
- *How does it taste, smell, and feel?*
- *Use your tone of voice to show enthusiasm and passion*

209

Now what usually happens is this, because I usually do this within a group exercise or interview, each of the teams is to stand at the front and describe their meals to the rest of the class. They then get scored out of 10 from the opposition (to be honest, this is just the jokey side of it for my own personal pleasure.)

You may be thinking that I have gone loopy, but this task alone does so much more than you think. To get really into your voice tone, you could also try taping your voice using your mobile phone etc and playing it back to give you a rough idea of where you need to practice on.

5 KEY ISSUES TO DO WITH COMMUNICATION

Hopefully you have carried out the task to the best of your ability, yes I know you may feel foolish or a 'right plum', but there is a reason I do this task and a whole lot more within class.

Can you think why this task is beneficial?

Like I have said earlier, I will never ask my learners to do anything I don't firmly believe would help them. I always say to the learners at the end; "*What does this task link to?*"

Well here are the reasons why I use this task:

1. Allows the learner to practice speaking with enthusiasm.
2. Brings the learner out of their comfort zone.
3. Gives them practice when speaking in front of an interviewer.
4. Gives them confidence with speaking in from of other people.
5. Allows them to develop their 'selling' skills by using key words.

So one little task can be used to cover 5 key issues with communication.

I just want to expand a little on the above list:

1. Speaking with enthusiasm needs to be practiced, especially if this is a *barrier* to gaining employment.
2. Coming out of our *comfort zone* is a major reason why many of us prefer to stay where we are. Un-employed or stuck in a job we don't like. We are scared by the unknown.
3. You need to practice talking to somebody about yourself and your skills; if you can do this task then talking to an interviewer will be much easier.
4. Speaking in front of a group of people will quite often shock an individual so they don't put themselves into that situation. What if you were at a group interview? You would need to do it then.
5. Develop your selling skills; this is what you then need to do. After all, you have just described food with enthusiasm and passion so you can sell your skills (to the interviewer) with the same tone, enthusiasm and passion.

Like I have said before, you may think that this is a pointless task, but the outcomes of doing this are worthwhile.

WHAT WE ACTUALLY SAY CAN MEAN NOTHING

What do I mean by this? Well if you are telling the interviewer all about your skills in a '*dull*' tone, then they are not even really listening to you. Again, picture that boring person who is telling you a great tale or story that has happened. What do you do? You turn off.

So I am not going to go into this much more. In a nutshell, you could be saying; "*I am going to go and collect my lottery winnings.*" But if you are that *boring* person then the person or persons you are talking to don't give a dam. They just want you out of their earshot. They are bored with you. Sorry, but that's how it is. And that is how it will be within your interview. You need to merge all three of the communication methods I have just gone over within your interview.

211

At the end of the day the majority of you will have (as mentioned earlier) on your C.V something which says you are a fantastic communicator and/or passionate individual with motivation and enthusiasm. Get this! If you get an interview, then you are onto a winner because they *like you*. So what do many of us do? Balls it up. Sorry for the language but we do. We sit there mumbling, have no idea what to say, cannot communicate effectively either individually or at different levels. Yes, you got it. A great big fat cross against your name.

Where is the passion? Where is the enthusiasm? Where has the excellent communicator gone? Down the 'swanny', that's where. And so have your chances of gaining employment or promotion etc. Honestly, please practice your communication technique. So what if you look daft talking to yourself. You will also look daft within the interview when they realise that what you have put on your C.V is not worthy of being your toilet roll.

I am actually getting quite angry at this point because I know it is where people fail and I really don't want any of you to. But, this *has* to come from within you. You need to get that self-belief and confidence, I know it's hard but look at the doors that will open up for you.

The opportunities that awaits you. Within my sessions my voice usually gets louder and louder as I really want to get the point across to the learners. Ask yourself this:

"Do I want to be that plastic rose all my life?"

Right, my finishing speech on this:

Get enthusiasm in your voice. Become passionate about the job. Be who you have put on your C.V. Become that confident person and believe in yourself. Because let me tell you:

"*The person in front or behind you at the interview will. Why should they get the job and not you? There's no reason what's so ever.*"

YOU DESERVE THAT JOB

Remember the filter I mentioned earlier? Well, if you cannot communicate effectively then you are going to be '*drop kicked*' out of the exit door.

RECAP AND CONSOLIDATION

Communication is the heart of getting it right, from your first impression within the interview to the way in which you sound all the way through it. Your body language could be saying:

"I am bored and don't really care whether I get the job or not"

But in fact we all know that this could be wrong, you could really be thinking:

"I am so relaxed and find the interview easy"

None of us can tell what the interviewer is thinking. Remember they are judging you, filtering you mentally in their own mind. They are looking at your body language to see if they can get extra information about you – even if this is totally wrong.
They may just go with their gut instincts, and that is not always good for the person being interviewed, especially if they have summed you up in a negative light.

> Brush up on your communication skills, ask somebody to help you with this and ask them for their honest opinion in how you come across.
>
> You could also ask somebody to try judging you on your body language at certain points throughout the day – when you don't realise they are taking notes.

YOUR PERSONAL NOTE PAGE

In the space below, write down any thoughts, ideas and notes you feel will help you throughout the book.

_____

_____

_____

_____

_____

_____

_____

_____

_____

_____

_____

_____

_____

_____

_____

_____

_____

215

STEP 10

INTERVIEW TECHNIQUES

AIM:	Develop your interview techniques, knowledge and skills within: (Group, Panel, One to One and Competency based Interviews).
OBJECTIVES:	By the end of this session you will be able to:

    ✓ Recognise 'killer questions'.

    ✓ Know the different kind of interviews used.

    ✓ Answer at least 50 questions.

    ✓ Demonstrate understanding of questions asked.

    ✓ Develop your interview responses within 3 seconds.

    ✓ Link all of previous sessions and skills learnt to the interview.

This is the end part of this long process and my favourite one. When I ask my learners to complete a feedback form at the end of their course, there is always a comment about the intense interview skills I give to the learners.

Any cards (of thanks) will almost certainly say something about their experience of interview techniques. This is because it is these techniques which will help you to secure that job!

Remember, the employer already likes you. They like what they have seen on your C.V so don't go spoiling it with a rubbish interview. I know you will be nervous, so would I, but think back to the positivity session and think;

"If I don't get this then okay, I will keep trying. What's the worst that could happen to me? It's all experience."

Too many people get paranoid about the interview, self doubt creeps in. I know, been there and got the bloody t – shirt. Get your mind into a routine of thinking:

"I am good at what I do and I know I will be an asset to any company and employer. I am just going to show them my passion and enthusiasm for wanting work."

I am going to say this all the way through this section: *"If you cannot communicate properly you will not get a job!"*

Let's get started.

INTERVIEW SELF CRITIQUE

Getting to know where you need to progress if you were to attend an interview is called being 'self aware'; you need to be aware of your weaker areas. Imagine your interview is the following day, how do you feel?

What area do you think you need to work on?

- Self belief

- Knowing enough about the company

- Communication/positive body language

- Answering the questions correctly

- Eye contact/Hand shaking

- Giving examples of own good practice

- Calming of nerves

- Other

Now be honest with yourself, if there are no areas that you need help with then you should quite easily get a job. If there are areas to improve on then have a think about how you can do it. This is about knowing where you need to develop further. Remember the title of the book? I am telling you how to get on the employment ladder. I told you that you already have the skills. And I am telling you again that you need to learn how to develop these skills.

Use the table below as a rough guide to help you criticise yourself and work on making them into positives (or use plain paper instead).

Self belief	
Knowing enough about the company	
Communication/positive body language	
Answering the questions correctly	
Eye contact/Hand shaking	
Giving examples of own good practice	
Calming of nerves	
Other	

"If you don't believe in yourself, then how the hell can you expect somebody else to believe in you? Take control and you will find work or get that promotion."

Tracey Morewood

IMPORTANT BASIC INTERVIEW GUIDELINES

Before I go in depth into the interview section I want you to take note of the guidelines listed below. Link this to all the other information and knowledge I am about to give you and your interview will have a positive outcome. I will bang on about this, but practice your body language for heaven's sake. Practice speaking at home on your own or with a partner etc. Who cares if you look at bit of a prat? If it means you are getting interviews and actually feeling positive and confident about yourself then so be it. Just go for it!

- Shake hands and introduce yourself – practice giving a nice firm handshake.
- Sit down when the interviewer/s ask you to.
- Be confident, they are really interested in you.
- Don't slouch; sit up with your back straight.
- Give clear answers, if you don't understand a question then just mention that you don't understand what they mean.
- Always give eye contact when answering a question.
- Listen to all questions.
- As you leave, shake hands and thank the interviewer/s for their time.
- Don't bad mouth previous employers or the company.
- Don't go into personal matters.
- Don't become arrogant with your answers.
- It's okay to have a sense of humour, but you must first have built up a rapport with the interviewer/s.
- Don't take hand written or typed out notes in with you.

221

THE KEY TO SUCCESSFUL INTERVIEWS

Think about what you would look for in a potential employee. What questions would you like to ask and what answers would you look for? I know we can never tell what is going to be asked. But do **research** on the company (aims, goals, values and mission) and ask yourself: *"How could I add value to the company?"*

Get a piece of paper and write down what **you** would ask **you** if **you** were the employer and interviewer. No that is not a limerick.

You need to know you. This is one of the keys to a successful interview. Right, let's get on with the rest of the interview skills.

SECRETS TO A FANTASTIC INTERVIEW

This is what you have been leading up to, getting to the interview stage. This is the end of the process I first mentioned. But remember, you need to get through the interview.

The biggest and one of the most important things I want you to understand is the answer to the next question.

What should you know before you sit before the interviewer?

You should know yourself, your skills and what you have to offer.

Another piece of advice I really need you take on board is that it is crucial to be able to answer at least 7 common interview questions (more later). I will expand on this when we get to it. To be able to answer these, you will need to develop your response. Once you have done this, you will sail through the interview.

222

Use the table below to tick off the statements in preparation for the interview. If you feel that you cannot tick at least six of these statements then you are not ready for the interview. Interview questions and the star approach will be explained in full details.

	✓	✗
You have researched the company and know what their mission statement, aims values and goals are.		
You believe you have something to offer the company with your skills.		
You appear confident in yourself, but not over confident.		
Your communication skills are excellent and you feel that you can communicate with a natural and friendly tone of voice.		
You are displaying enthusiasm, drive, passion and motivation when you speak and/or give examples of your past experience.		
You can answer any question they ask you (I will go through interview questions with you soon).		
You have read every section of this book and completed the 'self critique' table.		
You can back up everything that is on your C.V. Remember to be prepared to expand and explain things in detail (using the star approach – covered later).		
You are prepared for the interview – (journey time, interview clothes, where it is to be held, make an amazing positive first impression etc).		

All of these things you can do, we have gone over them within this book, should you feel that you are not ready, then re-read the sections you need to.

Please believe me when I say that if you take all of these things into consideration, your interview will go well. If it is that you don't get that job, then you can rest assured that it is not because you are not employable (because through reading this book you are), but there could have been somebody with more experience. The key here if you are unsuccessful, is to take the interview as a learning experience. Always ask for feedback on your interview, you may need to work on certain areas. So phone them and say that you would appreciate feedback.

INTERVIEWS CAN BE ACTUALLY QUITE NICE

Why are so many people scared when it comes to interviews? The biggest fear is not knowing. Not knowing how to answer the questions they may ask. Not knowing enough about the company. Let me tell you now, there is no reason at all why you should not know these things. If this is the case then you have wasted your time in reading this book, because you have not taken responsibility for your own actions. If you are serious about getting employment or gaining that promotion then you need to work harder.

Look at the skills you have developed. As you are aware, once you have developed something the key is to practice. See which parts of the book you need to go over and really give yourself a good talking to.

REAL EXAMPLES OF INTERVIEW EXPERIENCE

As I keep mentioning through this book, any examples are through real life experiences of people who I have worked with. The two examples below are from my own experience:

Looking to change my career direction I applied for a job role as a 'call centre representative'. How hard would it be, I can answer the telephone and put on a friendly voice. I passed the first stage which was a telephone interview, here they listened to what I had to say and the way in which I came across. I got through to the second stage; a mock phone call simulator. I was very nervous; believe me I wish I had the skills and knowledge I have given you back then.

A 'mock' customer phoned with a query and I had to help her with any question she asked. I then thought, "Right, I am going to try and sell her another product." Everybody else had finished their mock phone call and all ears were on me, I got even more nervous and began babbling. I forgot what the customer had initially phoned up for.

After 5 minutes two ladies came into the room and it was like an audition at X Factor. Five of us were taken to another room and we were told that they would not be taking the interview any further!

I was gutted. I felt stupid and humiliated. I felt rejected. All of the years studying to become a teacher and I could not even get a job answering telephones. I was shaking, crying and felt worthless. You may think this is a bit farfetched, I don't care. That's how I felt. How could I go for any other job knowing that I could not get that one?

I phoned the company up the next day for feedback; they told me that if I had researched the company I would have found out that 'selling' products is not their main aim. Keeping the customer happy is!

225

So I had a choice. Do I remain in my current job role which I had begun to lose faith in? Or brush myself down, take a deep breath and continue searching for another job?

I didn't really know what I wanted to do; all I knew was that I got immense pleasure in teaching and making a difference. Then I came across a job vacancy as am Employability Tutor and I thought, "why the hell not." Now, you need to remember that this is not something I had a great deal of experience in, I was used to doing this within the prison environment, but I tried anyway.

I have given you another example of my own interview experience for the role of 'Employability Tutor'.

So here I am all prepared for the interview, I knew the mission statement inside and out. I tailored my answers in my own mind to try and get in keywords from their own statement and goals. Read the example on the next page.

My Competency based interview:

I put myself inside the shoes of the interviewers (it was a panel interview too), what are they likely to ask me? I arrived early, well 1 ½ hours to be precise. And I was a nervous wreck. Part of the job role was to have a good understanding on the 'labour market'. What the hell was that about? But do you know, I read through this large document about the labour market (whilst sat outside a cafe and chain smoking) and thought to myself; "I have a lot to offer this company and I know I am good at what I do (and secretly hoped they wouldn't ask about the labour market too much)." So I washed the fag smell away, ate a mint on my way to the interview and felt confident in myself (well I told myself that I was anyway).

I smiled politely at everyone I met within the office where the interview was to take place. I then was called in and shook the hands of the interviewers and as I sat down they started asking me questions. How do I overcome barriers to learning? How do I include everyone within class? What are my opinions on Equality and Diversity? The list went on and on, but do you know what? Half way through I realised that I was actually enjoying this. I knew what I could do. I knew how I could add value (yes, after practising). I knew that just given a chance I would be able to prove myself. So after the interview I went home really happy, so much different from the previous week. I should have heard something within 5 days but I had not heard anything. I thought, "*frigging hell, I could not have done anything more in the interview.*" But what I took away from it was experience and felt that the next interview would be easier.

227

I phoned the company back after a week to ask for feedback. I was told that "*I was like a breath of fresh air.*" They were now in a position to offer me the post.

So, enough about me, but I hope you realise that going to an interview needn't be a scary affair – ok it's not going to be all chilled out and laid back every time you attend one. But you need to remember that an employer wants to see your personality too.

What I have since learnt about that interview is that one of the major things that I did was speak with passion and enthusiasm. I gave great examples to each question they asked me, which they found really positive too.

Okay, we have covered some important basic bits, again, I am going to keep saying this but you *must* keep reading about body language. Don't cock up your interview because of this, believe in yourself and I guarantee you will feel so much more confident.

Remember on earlier sessions I mentioned about your tone of voice, well this is where you will need to practice even more because we are getting close to those all important interview questions.

Part of the process of securing that job is by being put through a *filtering system*. You won't see this filter because the majority of the time, the filter is in the minds of the interviewer/s.

So keep this in mind:

"Don't give them any excuse to filter you out of the door without a job offer."

Yes, you may not get the job but that could be for other reasons. Don't *you* be the one to do the filtering for them by answering questions wrong: in a negative manner, displaying negative body language, lacking confidence, not understanding your own skills etc?

Here we are with the lovely filter again. Look at the opportunities throughout the book in which we can be filtered through our own actions. So even more effort is needed as we go through more interview skills.

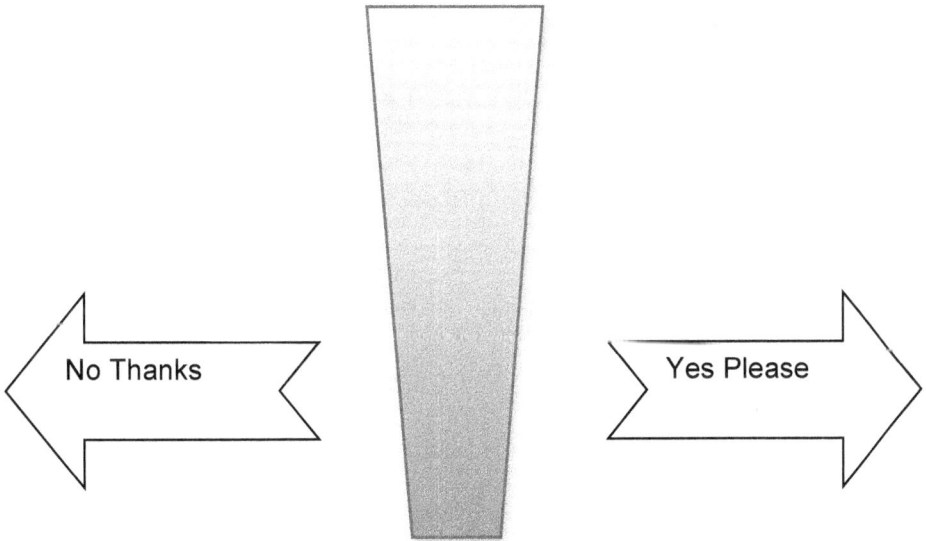

No Thanks

Yes Please

229

How To Be Successful In A Group Interview

The first thing you need to ask yourself is why? Why do companies have group interviews? So have a think. Have you ever been to a group interview? If you have then what did you do?

The main purpose of a group interview is to interview on 'mass', interview more than one person. This could range from 6 – 60 people in one interview. This amount is a rough estimate but basically there will be quite a few people attending. Time and money can be a key factor for companies to hold group interviews, especially if they are recruiting for a new site or for a large number of workers. This is due to the fact that everyone and everything has a monetary value; especially when it comes down to a business. And everybody's' time is valuable.

I mentioned filtering earlier; this could also be used for other reasons. Group interviews could also be used to *filter* out people before a one to one or panel interview. This is usually called *stages*; you may have to go through stages to get to the final interview.

You may not know beforehand that your interview is a *group interview*, so after reading this section you will be prepared.

In the space below, write down what you think an employer looks for during this type of interview:

_____

_____

_____

_____

25 POINTS TO CONSIDER WITHIN A GROUP INTERVIEW

I hope you managed to list some points. Well here a few other points:

1. How do you communicate
2. Your personality
3. Positive and negative body language
4. The way in which you work
5. How are you with other people
6. Are you a team player
7. Are you tolerant of others
8. Do you listen to other views
9. Can you lead a team
10. Can you motivate a team
11. Are you able to support others
12. Can you follow instructions
13. Are you aware of basic health and safety
14. Are you aware of equality and diversity
15. Can you facilitate a group of people
16. Are you able to delegate tasks
17. Are you considerate to others
18. How do you interact others
19. Can you work as a team to solve problems
20. How organised are you
21. Do you prioritise and plan effectively
22. Can you handle stressful situations
23. Are you influential
24. Do you show respect to different points of view
25. Are you laid back, let somebody else do the work

The employer may have different ideas on why they are holding a group interview; they may be looking for a specific talent or ability.

AUDITIONS AND NOT INTERVIEWS

Have you ever tried joining TGI Friday? I will give you an example on the experience one of my learners had there in a moment. If you get a chance take a look around their website (full web address at the end of the book), you should notice under **Join Us** the following: *If you'd like to audition (we don't do interviews!) then click here.*

This is a clear indication that, should you have an audition (interview), then it isn't going to be a typical interview. You should be warned; you will most likely be observed and judged from the start. As soon as you enter the room! You may also be given a set time of when you need to have completed all of the set tasks. If you and your group have finished early then remember you are still being observed. Put more effort into your part of the activity and/or discuss with the group any improvements you could make (make sure you use all of your allocated time wisely).

One of my learners went to an interview at TGI's and she said, "It was really good, it didn't even feel like an interview. I had a really good time."

She said that the interview was a *group interview* and she kept going over everything I had gone through the previous week. The outcome was that she gained full time employment. The bonus part (and motivation for me) was that her friend also attended the interview and had no idea on how to behave. My learner informed me that she quickly gave her guidance on what I had previously said. Result, her friend also gained employment.

So what tasking jobs and problem solving skills were involved? Well in this particular instance my learner had to play: Jenga and Twister. Yes that's right, board games. Other people had similar games and activities to complete. So why do you think they had to play board games and fun activities?

- To see their personalities.
- How they interact with others.

232

- Can they quickly adapt to situations?
- Their interpersonal skills.
- Patience.
- Remain stress free.
- Are they willing to get involved?

Now, the *sting* in the tail here is that each group was made up of around 6 – 8 people. One of the group members within each of the groups was a manager or team leader within the company. What these people did was pretend they too where *auditioning* and they asked questions to other members of the group about what they knew about TGI's. A bit similar to 'Undercover Boss' or to a 'Mystery Shopper'.

What an ingenious way to interview. They see the real person, their real qualities and values. And as I have said before, they can really see through a person who is displaying negative **body language**. But there are certain things you need to watch out for during a group interview. A list of 'what to do' and 'What not to do' is really important.

WHAT YOU 'SHOULD' OR 'SHOULD NOT' DO WITHIN A GROUP INTERVIEW?

Put your own thoughts down here (or on separate paper).

What to do in a group interview	What not to do in a group interview

233

Here I have given you a list of what I would take into consideration at a group interview:

What to do in a group interview
Smile
Let your personality shine through
Display positive body language
Communicate effectively throughout
Try and include quieter members
Be natural
Get involved
Give your opinions
Show respect to others
Turn up on time
Listen and follow instructions
Be friendly
Create a great first impression
Introduce yourself to your group
Be confident, but not arrogant
Contribute to all aspects of the task
Research the company before attending
Give eye contact throughout
Make sure you are looking smart and clean
Support others
Prepare to answer interview questions
Have a couple of questions ready to ask the interviewers

As you can see the list is quite long, but I assure you, take these into account and you will do well within your group interview.
I will say this again:

"If you cannot communicate effectively, then your chances of getting a job are very limited if not rare."

A ROTTEN WAY TO FILTER

Have you seen some of the *Ice Breakers* during your learning experience at all? Well these are sheets of paper with around 20 random questions on such like:

1. How many days of the week have a 'Y' in them?
2. What gets wetter the more you use it?

Pointless questions. But if you were to look closer you will see in smaller letters the instructions:

Please read the following questions carefully before starting this exercise.

Then at around question 18 you will be asked to Ignore the rest of the questions and just put your name on the sheet.

What is the point of the task? To see if you can follow instructions and carry them out carefully. And let me tell you, this has been carried out in a couple of group interviews to filter people out. I have often used this to get the point across how easy it is to allow ourselves to be filtered out of the door. When I perform a group interview I give each group member a task sheet. The important task here is to **read** the instructions first. I then observe throughout and give feedback to each group and where necessary to each individual. You may think you have nothing to worry about because you have ticked all of the boxes about how to perform well. Be warned!

235

It is quite easy to feel too comfortable during this type of interview and quite often people do the some of the following:

What not to do in a group interview
Swear
Look bored and un-interested
Display negative body language
Not listen to other people's views
Don't communicate with quieter members
Show off when an observer walks by
Arrive late
Become over confident and arrogant
Make inappropriate comments
Make racial remarks or offending remarks
Dress as a scruff
Yawn all the way through
Roll up a cig for when they have a break
Don't give any opinion, view or support to the task
Chew gum
Mess with your hair and make-up
Belittle and/or put down others
Walk with an attitude or swagger
Mess about with your phone
Become easily distracted

As you can see there are a lot of things what you shouldn't do. And let me inform you, almost all of these listed above are examples of what people have done when I do the 'mock interviews'. My learners will also give me examples of their own experience and this list of 'what not to do' usually means that there is always someone who will slip up.

ONE THING YOU SHOULD ALWAYS THINK AND CONSIDER?

Your *group interview* is still:

AN INTERVIEW

So many tales I have heard about how people have behaved and not taken this kind of interview serious.

Remember that also this group interview could just be a *filter*, to see which candidates they want to take to the next stage of the interview process. In my experience most group interviews don't focus too much on asking questions as they could be asked at the next stage. But again, always prepare yourself for any question, and *always* research the company beforehand.

Are you quite a loud person? I am, I will be honest. I am usually the joker of a group, if you answered 'yes' to this question then be careful. Take a close look at yourself. Do you stand out for the wrong reasons? I know that if I was going to a group interview, I would need to think about my approach. Yes, I do have a bubbly personality but does that come across as that I don't take things seriously? I do know that I can quite easily take over and lead tasks, this is a good point to have, but do I come across as controlling?

"Stand out for the right reasons, not for the wrong reasons."

Over the next few pages we will look at the way in which you can answer questions using the *star* approach – especially if you are having a *competency* based interview.

THE KEY TO ANSWERING WITH THE STAR APPROACH

To be able to fully 'back up' your C.V, to answer interview questions to the best of your ability, then I would say have a look at the *'star'* approach. By using this approach to answer any question the interviewer/s may ask will make you look and sound *competent*. This will also allow you to be even more confident within a *competency based interview.*

This type of interview means that you need to expand on all of your answers in a way that shows you are competent in that area. This is really easy to do, but again, you must first do your homework. If you think competent as been *'able'*, then all you are doing is telling your interviewer how you are able to carry out tasks.

238

STAR

S	T	A	R
I	A	C	E
T	S	T	S
U	K	I	U
A		O	L
T		N	T
I			
O			
N			

Now let me break that down even further.

When answering a question always explain to the interviewer/s the following:

1. What was the situation
2. What was the task or job you had to do
3. What action or what did you do throughout the task
4. What was the end result

YOUR PERSONAL SKILLS

Think about your qualities which you have wrote down on your CV (team work, communication skills, problem solving, works on own initiative - etc). List your personal skills and provide evidence to back up your CV.

239

SKILL	EVIDENCE
EXAMPLE: *Works well in a team.*	*I supported a team of pickers and packers to ensure orders were dispatched efficiently and accurately.*

Think about how you will communicate this back when you are in an actual interview. Again, you will see that I am getting you to list or write down what you have done and when. What was the result? How can you evidence it? This is the key of getting to know your own skills and to claim what you have done.

By doing these tasks will certainly make you a strong candidate for any job you are applying for, because you are coming across as competent and able.

This task will lead us onto using the star approach, you will notice that they are similar but you first need to know the evidence of your skills before you can apply them with the star approach.

I am giving you a task below and I want you to answer the following questions using the *star approach*.

1. Think of an example when you used teamwork to get a job done.

2. Think of an incident when you communicated effectively to get a good outcome.

3. When have you used your own initiative?

4. When have you gone that extra mile for someone?

5. Describe a time when you have been really motivated about something.

6. What are you passionate about?

7. You say you are good with people, give me an example of this.

Rather than me going through each of the questions I will give you a couple of examples of the above. This again is where you need to take ownership, if these questions don't relate to your area then make some up yourself and test yourself on how you respond using the star approach.

Response to:

Question 1
This response came when I helped out at a recruitment day, and often occurs when I do one to one interviews:

I use teamwork every day!

That was it. No explanation, nothing. Not good enough. As an interviewer this told me that the candidate did not really have relevant experience nor did they come across as competent. Straight away in the interviewers' mind, you would have a big fat cross at the side of your name for that question.

241

A more typical and acceptable response would be:

Whilst working as a warehouse operative it was really important that the delivery vans go out of the yard for 10 pm. To ensure this happened, me and my colleagues would work together to carefully load the van in the correct way and double check each others' paper work.
By using team work we made sure that if any errors had to be amended then we could get this done quickly and efficiently. Once this had been done and all of the paper work signed the driver always departed the depot on time. The result of this great team work was that the receiver of the goods always had their stock at the allocated time, and the customer would get their products at the specific time given.

Response to:

Question 4
This was actually my response when I had a telephone interview.

"When I was working as a retail manager, one lady came to me really excited. She had found a pair of shoes that would finish off her wedding outfit. When I looked for her size I found that we did not have her size in stock. I phoned around other stores, but the customer did not have transport to get to these stores. I explained that if she could call back in after dinner time the next day, I would travel to the store after I had finished work and fetch them back for the lady to try on. The customer called back the next day, and the shoes fit her perfectly. She could not thank me enough. She became a valued and loyal customer."

Although the majority of the response was true, I did expand and exaggerate (some may say lie slightly). The outcome from the interviewer at the other end of the phone was: *'fantastic and excellent answers'*. Now I don't want to tell you to lie, but expanding on your answer shows the interviewer that you are competent and you are able to do your job to a good standard. They aren't going to exactly phone this mysterious lady up now are they?

But I had to do my own homework. I realised that this company really did value their customers, so to get to the next stage of the interview I had to make sure that my answers were tailored all about meeting the needs of the customer.

So remember that when you are asked a question, use the **star** method. This will make you appear competent and able.

Now, look at your C.V. What have you put on it? Are you an excellent communicator and if so prove it? Are you willing to go above and beyond for the customer and the company? If so give specific examples. Do you see yourself as a team player – why? So as you can see, we are now using the knowledge from previous sessions. As I said in those sessions – become and know your C.V. Prepare to be asked about your C.V and always have a response ready in the star approach.
Take ownership and practice!

How To Sail Through The Panel Interview

How many of you have had a panel interview? A panel interview consists of a few interviewers (usually two, three or four). I have experienced three of these types of interviews and they can be quite stressful if you haven't done your homework or research.

What usually happens with this kind of interview is that one interviewer will ask the questions, one will be making notes and the other person could also fire questions at you. Interviewers will most likely have their questions ready, they are not trying to catch you out, but if you do your homework and know what you are about and believe in yourself then you will be fine.

My first taste of a panel interview consisted of three people. I knew these people already as this was a promotion I was going for. But don't let that fool you, these people grilled me. But because I knew my job, because I knew I was a great worker and because I knew my own skills, strengths and abilities I ended up getting the position I applied for.

What happens usually, or certainly in the case I have just mentioned above, each person was asking questions and rating my answer with a **score** out of 10.

The three interviewers then discussed the answers given and if I had scored low in a particular important area then that would be one black cross against my name. I ended up getting the job promotion. But it didn't end there; I will go more into this in a while.

Now, with me being a bit nosey and curious, a couple of weeks later I asked somebody about the scoring system as I wanted to know how I did.

The feedback I got was excellent, and certainly a turning point for me. I always believe I can do better, and certainly lack self belief at times. But I was told that I answered about four questions on the list with just one answer; this is because I gave explanations and examples to *back up* my knowledge. And no, it wasn't because I was rambling either (because I can). The turning point for me and one in which I will always remember, is when the Manager said that one of the questions that they left out was:

"What gives you motivation and enthusiasm?"

She explained that there was no point in asking the question as I had demonstrated that all the way through with the way I communicated and with my positive body language and with the enthusiasm in my responses.

My next taste of a panel interview was also positive, I got that job too. Now, although the questions were asked, this time I was not scored. This time the interviewers made notes against statements and a criteria already printed out on a document.

How close were my answers?

They were looking for a particular answer for each of the questions and they wrote down my response on this document. This can be very off putting.

So if you find yourself in this position, ignore the fact that the interviewers are writing loads of notes. You need to focus. You need to listen to the questions and explain fully what you mean. Therefore, you will be making sure you have actually covered some, if not all of the criteria to which the interviewers will be working from.

I mentioned on the previous page that after I got my promotion that it didn't end there. Well I had also gone for another position – a higher position than I had ever worked. So two hours after getting the first job promotion I had to have another interview. This time, people came from other establishments. By this time my nerves were in shreds. Not only did I have another panel interview, I had to give a presentation (cannot remember the title). This can be another way in which you are interviewed. Presenting information, with this I needed to draw on all of my communication skills, knowledge and strengths and abilities. At the end of the interview the Manager asked; *"So Tracey, do you still want the job?"* I replied with; *"No."* You should have seen the look on their faces, but I knew this position just wasn't for me so I told them I didn't want the job anymore.

Afterwards the Manager informed me that I would have got the job, but I just didn't feel ready for that kind of responsibility. Maybe it was my lack of self belief, lack of confidence in my abilities. I don't know, but I do know that I have never regretted that decision. I have just looked at things as opportunities.

So although panel interviews can seem daunting, they are just the same as a one to one interview. You need to believe in yourself, you need to ooze enthusiasm and motivation. You need to be competent and get across that you are able to carry out any task, and if you don't know how to do a task then you will just learn.

245

If you are asked to give a presentation (this usually happens when you go for a managerial or team leader role), then use all of the skills I have taught you and research the company. You will be given a title of your presentation but you also need to know what the company goals and values are. Once you have found this information out you need to adapt your presentation slightly to link with what the company or organisation is about. If the presentation has no significance with their aims and values etc, then leave it. But try and get this across in the way in which you answer your questions.

REMEMBER: KNOWLEDGE IS POWERFUL

If you are seeking to move higher within a company or moving to a different company to seek progression within you, then one tool I want you to have is *knowledge*. If you have knowledge about a company then they will love you already. Remember, knowledge can be powerful if used correctly.

Put yourself in the shoes of the interviewer/s again. They have interviewed three people already and nobody has yet *stood out*, then in you come. You now have a wealth of *employability skills* to offer, and then you're asked a *'killer'* interview question:

(Interview within the Education Sector): *"Why should we choose you?"*

This is your moment to shine. This is where you sock it to them. This is where you are going to stand out from the crowd. My example response to this would be along the lines of:

"I have the skills and abilities to help you carry out your mission statement of 'creating learning opportunities to those that need it the most'; I would do this by helping to break down the individuals' barrier to learning, listening and putting the learner at the heart of what I do. Through embedding 'soft skills' and building up a respectful relationship I will get the best out of the learner and the learner would most certainly get the best out of the company. Hopefully you have seen that I am passionate about helping others and that I am motivated in helping the company to move forward. That is why I think you should choose me."

246

I know it is quite long and wordy, so what. You have been asked a question and you are giving them the answer that they would love to hear. Yes, you need to make sure that the passion and enthusiasm is there in your voice and body language. You need to mean what you say (well almost). This is the model answer for this situation. This has now made you stand out from the crowd. You have rubbed their **ego**; you have shown that you have taken time to actually look at their statements and goals. Do not ramble though. Be specific to the needs of the company and the job role.

If you believe in yourself and your skills then this will roll off your tongue fluently. After all, you don't want to sound like a robot when you're speaking. They will see through this straight away.

So what do you need to do?

Believe that you are good, that you are just as good as the next person.

Believe that you are of value, but most of all you need to believe in the skills you do have and 'sell' yourself in a positive way.

This is why it is important to make sure you read the positivity and motivation section.

247

COMMON INTERVIEW QUESTIONS

Question Time Activity:

To prepare you for your interviews, you first need to be ready for some of the common interview questions which you could be asked. I mentioned earlier that I will help you to develop your knowledge of your own skills. Well, from the questions below, seven of these you already have the answers to.

Q1. Tell me about yourself.

Q2. Why did you apply for this role?

Q3. What are your strengths?

Q4. What salary do you expect?

Q5. Where do you see yourself in 5 years time?

Q6. Do you have any weaknesses?

Q7. Are you motivated within work?

Q8. What makes you the best candidate for this job?

Q9. Are there any question/s would you like to ask us?

Q10. How would your friends describe you in three words?

I have given examples of what to include in your response and why you may be asked these questions in the first place.

KNOW WHY YOU MAY BE ASKED CERTAIN QUESTIONS

Some employers have a motive for asking certain questions, some don't. But I want to just go through some of the questions I gave you on the previous page:

Q1. Tell me about yourself.

*Quite often, this is asked to get you to relax more so that your true personality shines through your nerves. Don't tell them that you're a raving beer monster who loves to party. No I am not talking about myself here – Um, let's move on. Is there something on their website that you could link to? Make it all positive, but remember your **tone** of voice they will want to hear passion and enthusiasm. You will need to know about yourself here.*

Q2. Why did you apply for this role?

Do you feel that you have all the relevant skills they are asking for? Do you see yourself working for the company and adding value? This may be asked to see if you know anything good about the company, why did you apply for a role with this company? Again, stroke their ego. Tell them through researching it you have found it to be something you believe in. Or, do you know somebody who has or is working there and you have heard excellent things about it. Are you an existing customer of the company? If so, tell them which products you use and why you like them.

Q3. What are your strengths?

If you say, "Um, I don't really know." Then you are telling them really that you don't actually have any. What is on your C.V? What are your key skills/abilities/achievements? What's your Personal Profile? This is where you will find your strengths.

249

Q4. What salary do you expect?

I hate this one. I have been asked a similar question to this before. Be confident. If there was a salary advertised with the job, then say that. If it was a salary between £... and £..., explain that you are open to negotiations. If in doubt at all, just say you are willing to discuss this.

Q5. Where do you see yourself in 5 years time?

I love this question, this is easy. So many people get it wrong and say; "I would love to start my own business." Or "Still doing what I am doing really." No. The reason this question is being asked is to see numerous things: Are you motivated and self motivated, do you want to progress, have you got drive and ambition. Let me tell you now, if you are ever asked this question then be careful, in 5 years time you should say that if you were successful at the interview, then you would love to see yourself progress within the company. No employer wants to hire an individual, train them to a good standard, and invest money in their training only for them to leave for another company.

Q6. Do you have any weaknesses?

Another one I hate. Make sure you can think of at least one weakness. I know it contradicts me telling you to be confident about your skills and now I am asking you to state your weaknesses. But again, this is asked for a reason. You could be asked this question to see if you're self-aware. This means that you are aware of where you need to improve or work harder on. When I was asked this question I replied that Maths used to be my weakness, but through determination I went to college and gained my level 2 in this subject. I could hardly say; "A pint of lager and a bag of onion rings," could I? Don't be too honest here though. Don't say something like, "I hate speaking to other people, I prefer to work on my own."

This has been said before and in my experience and you're straight off their list. This same person then had on their C.V 'enjoys working as part of a team.' They can see right through you.

250

Q7. Are you motivated within work?

If you say, "I suppose, it just depends on the job." Then the outcome will be; 'Goodbye'. Every employer wants their staff to be motivated, regardless of their job. If you are not motivated this will pass on through the workforce. Have a think, have you ever worked with somebody that always complains about their work? They end up de-motivating you; this then has a knock on effect to the company. So for this explain what motivates you; getting the best out of each task you do because you know you do it to the best of your ability. Again, depending on the company (research values, aims and goals etc), and focus on what they are about. This is especially true if it involves working in retail. Helping meet the demands of the customer could be a clear motivation for you.

Q8. What makes you the best candidate for this job?

I love this question. But this is only because when I was asked this question I really nailed it to them. Again, I knew what I had to offer and how I had inspired a great deal of people over the years. Also, I believed in myself and this shone through with my answers. So, if you are ever asked this question, prepare to knock their shoes off with your reply. Again, it is your turn to shine and to give the interviewers the confidence to hire you. Remember though, there is a fine line between confident and over confident (arrogant springs to mind).

Q9. Are there any question/s would you like to ask us?

How many of you have been asked this question and then said, "No, you have covered everything?" Wrong. Always have a question ready, it shows that you are interested in the company and that you want to find out more. But, don't ask about the salary and wage rises. Once you have been offered the position then mention the money (odds are that you already know about the salary anyway).

Q10. How would your friends describe you in three words?

The interviewer wants to hear how you react to this question. So have a think, and don't be too honest. If they would normally say that you can me miserable, snappy and hardworking then you have blown it. Yes the hardworking part is good, but the other two are not good traits to advertise within your interview. Think of some other great words to use. What about linking it to the job and what they are looking for?

What did you think of those questions? If you thought they were hard, then just wait for the competency based questions! As mentioned earlier, the competence interview is designed for you to show how *competent* you are, and how you will fit into the company's structure. Below I have given a few competency based questions, there are literally loads. I am going to go through the ones that I have either experienced or previous clients have experienced.

A skill here is to use the *star* approach. So think of a situation and break it down, that way you will come across as able and competent. Again, research their website and get as much information as you can. Can you link your answers to both your own experiences and to the needs' of the company?

COMPETENCY BASED QUESTIONS

Have a look at the competency based questions below and spend about 30 minutes looking through them and thinking of a situation:

1. Tell us about a situation where your communication skills made a difference to a situation?

"Whilst working for my previous employer, I had to liaise with the learner, team-leader and manager in providing a solution in making the resources learner friendly. I gave input into what was wrong and how I felt we could make things better. I put my ideas into practice and the result was that the success rate of the course was 100% whilst I was in charge of it. The team-leader and manager then put this same practice into another two courses, making these successful too.

2. Describe a situation where you had to deal with an angry customer.

Within my role as retail assistant I had to calm down an angry customer who was not happy with a product she had bought. Straight away I changed the tone of my voice to show empathy and understanding. I informed the customer that we had not had any problems with this product, but I would either give her a full refund or exchange the product. The customer walked away from the shop a happy customer and continued to shop with us again and again.

3. Describe a situation where you had a disagreement or an argument with management or colleague. How did you handle it?

When I was working as a Warehouse Operative I was informed that my picking figures were not good enough. I explained that I had only just had a review with my line-manager the previous day and they had told me that I had exceeded my targets. I then continued to explain that I had taken their concerns on board and I would seek to improve my performance. The result in this matter was that they had miscalculated my morning's work they apologised and thanked me for my co-operation.

4. Describe a time where you failed to sell an idea at work.

Example 1: I cannot recall a time where I have failed to sell an idea because my manager has confidence in my ability to get the job done to a high standard and on time.

Example 2: I informed my manager that I would move certain products to another part of the store to maximise sales. I told him that due to the season it would attract more customers into the store. His reply was; "It looks okay where it is."

5. How do you deal with stress?

It's rare that I ever get stressed because I would ask for support and/or help before it got to that stage. Due to my organisation and prioritising skills I would always try and give my best, but if I felt that this was not enough then I would seek to find a solution.

6. Give us an example of a situation where you worked under pressure.

Because of the nature of my previous job role, and with targets to meet and goal posts been moved on a daily basis I often find I work even better under pressure. Because of my enthusiasm and drive, quite often this pressure just pushes me more to succeed.

7. Describe a situation in which you were a member of team. What did you do to positively contribute to it?

I am a great believer in working as a team and I do so every day. One particular situation arose in which me and my work mates needed to load a wagon for 10 pm. I noticed that my friend was struggling with her cage of items and gave her support to complete her job quicker. Because we were waiting for this cage of items the wagon was not on course to go out at the allocated time slot. To ensure this didn't happen, six people worked non-stop in securing the cage, creating labels and entering it on the computer system. The result was that the wagon kept to its time scale and all of the goods would be delivered on time.

8. How do you build relationships with other members of your team?

I feel that by giving support, listening to their ideas and communicating effectively is a great way in building relationship within a team. As you can see from my previous answer, a great relationship has formed with working as a team.

Can you see how I have used the *star approach* as much as I could to answer the questions? Could you also see that by expanding on my answers I actually answered more than one question?

This shows that I am competent in my work; I know what I am talking about. Practice, practice and more practice.

COMPETENCY BASED WRONG ANSWERS

Using the same questions I am going to give you some more examples, except this time these are *common wrong answers*. These answers are what I hear time and time again. Know yourself, know your skills and know what the job entails.

It can often just take one answer to mess up your interview. Be prepared beforehand so this is not the case. Remember, once you have said your answer, there is no going back. Quite often we may say something daft because we are embarrassed because we don't know what to say. Again, I have been there and started laughing to cover up my own nerves. Didn't work though; luckily my interviewers were quite nice and actually saw the funny side. I would not recommend this tactic though.

Let's have a look at some common wrong answers then:

1. Tell us about a situation where your communication skills made a difference to a situation?

When I asked my boss to get somebody to look after the till because I was due a break.

2. Describe a situation where you had to deal with an angry customer.

I always shout for the manager to come and sort it out, that's what they get paid for.

3. Describe a situation where you had a disagreement or an argument with management or colleague. How did you handle it?

I tried not to let the disagreement escalate so I told the women in question that I would sort it out after work hours.

4. Describe a time where you failed to sell an idea at work.

I have never been in that situation; I'm just the cleaner so they would not ask me anyway.

5. How do you deal with stress?

I would go outside for a cigarette and calm down or I have often gone into a room and asked people to leave me alone for 5 minutes.

6. Give us an example of a situation where you worked under pressure.

When my manager went on holiday. I had to help run the shop and I could not do it. We ended up shutting it up an hour earlier each day to get caught up. The shop always looked nice the next day for the early morning customer.

7. Describe a situation in which you were a member of team. What did you do to positively contribute to it?

Just when I was on the conveyor belt at the meat factory, one person would put the things on the belt and I would just take them off! (This is not too bad, but you would need to expand more).

8. How do you build relationships with other members of your team?

I will speak to them once I get to know them.

There are far too many questions to put down, and we will never know what questions the interviewers are likely to ask. One thing I do know is that the higher the position you are going for, the harder the questions are going to be.

So what, you will manage it. Look at the job specification and work on your star approach.

OTHER COMPETENCE QUESTIONS YOU COULD BE ASKED! AND WHY!

Some of the reasons why an employer would ask the competence questions are:

- Are you able to contribute as part of a team?
- Are you aware of other people, sensitive to their needs and situations?
- Able to deal with pressure and how?
- Do you have a flexible approach and are you adaptable?
- You can make decisions and explain your reasons why?
- Can you diffuse situations, if not what would you do?

1. Describe a situation in which you were a member of a team. What did you do to positively contribute to it?

2. How do you ensure every member of the team is allowed to participate?

3. When did you last upset someone?

4. What do you think makes you impatient at work?

5. Tell us about your biggest failure. How did you move on from it?

6. Describe a situation where you were asked to do something that you have never attempted previously.

7. What is the decision that you have put off for the longest?

8. Tell me about a time when your communication skills have made a difference to a situation.

9. What place does empathy play in your work? Give an example where you needed to show empathy.

10. How do you deal with conflict?

257

Again, there is no point in putting down my own responses here; you need to think about what you do in and out of work. What situation can you come up with to help you answer those questions?

Re-read the good and the not so good responses. If you were the employer and interviewer, which candidate would you go for after reading the responses? Why have you chosen them?

Hopefully you could see how competent and able the candidate was who was answering the first questions. Whilst reading the common wrong responses, what was your thought?

Do you think I have made them up? Let me tell you, when I have done one to one interviews, recruitment events and panel interviews, then these responses become very common. Yes, looking at them now it looks like common sense not to answer the questions like that. But people do.

Hopefully, you're not going to be one of these people. If you think you could be, read the blooming book again.

UNDERSTANDING 'KILLER' QUESTIONS

Depending on the type of job you are going for, you could be asked what's called a 'killer' question. They usually ask this type of question for two reasons:

1. To get to know how you think, never under estimate how much information we can give away about ourselves when asked a killer question.

   or

2. They are just plain evil! Not really, but if you're going for a managerial/team leader role then be *more* prepared for this type of questioning.

So, let's have a look at just a few killer questions.

258

Why did you choose to apply to our company?

This is really testing to see if you know anything about their company. This is also your time to shine and sell yourself and your personality. Remember, what makes you stand out from everybody else.

What haven't I asked you that you wish I had?

Not a trick question, how well have you prepared for the interview and how ready you are to sell yourself and your skills. Try and think of a really hard question that would really make the interviewer/s sit up and listen.

Have you read our values? How could you help us to achieve these?

Yes I know you now know all about these, but make sure you do before you attend any interview. The interviewer is waiting for compliments here. Remember their ego?

When did you last feel out of your comfort zone? How did you feel?

Here they could be looking to see if you are up for a challenge, and adaptable in working within other areas without having a panic attack.

What gets you out of bed in a morning?

Don't snigger and say something inappropriate; (even though it could be funny). They want to see your enthusiasm, motivation and passion for work.

YOUR ONE TO ONE INTERVIEW AND THE 3 SECOND RULE

If you have somebody at home or at work to help you then great. If not, no worries just practice saying your replies out loud. Again, be self critical of your answers, could you do better? Do you need to think too long before you feel you can answer? You should aim to start with your response within *three* seconds. Any longer then the interviewer could begin to doubt your ability. Try counting to three; it is quite a long time really. Now try counting to five, there is too long of a pause.

This is preparing you. This is getting down to what could actually be a *successful interview*. I recommend that you read all of the questions out loud. Take your time and for each one try and answer using the star approach where necessary. Remember that the interviewer wants to get to know what *you* know. So the key here is to:

"Know yourself
Sell yourself
Be aware of yourself"

Tracey Morewood

By knowing your own skills, strengths and abilities you are immediately in a fantastic position. With this knowledge you will then become more relaxed and your natural passion and enthusiasm should shine through the nerves. Again, if you cannot and do not communicate effectively and display positive body language throughout then you are filtering yourself out of the exit door.

To get the most out of this one to one interview it helps if you base your answers around the type of job you would normally be looking for. The key to a successful interview is also knowing enough information about the company beforehand. Remember those aims, values, goals and mission statements? Well what is the company about? What is their passion? I would recommend that you target at least five companies which you would like to work for and research them. With your information, tailor some of the questions to what the company is about.

260

"Knowledge is a powerful tool,
Use all of the information you have as your power.
Use the knowledge of yourself as your special tool."

TURNING AROUND NEGATIVE SITUATIONS

Here I am going to highlight some interview questions that could be met with a negative response. They don't need to be.

I asked the question earlier: *"What are your weaknesses"?* This question seems to be the most daunting one to answer. We don't want to admit our weakness, but this question could also be worded differently. There are many questions you would dread being asked, but with the knowledge you can overcome them. The skill here is not to feed them with a massive list of weaknesses. Turn any negative point into a positive response; it could be that the interviewer is just *testing* you to see how you handle the question. So get the knowledge beforehand, make a note of at least two weaknesses and think about the steps you have or are making to overcome these.

YOU HAVEN'T GOT ALL THE SKILLS

Remember I told you to go for the job role even if you don't have all of the relevant skills? So if you're asked, *"What experience have you had"?* You need to start your response off in a positive way. Make sure you inform them that even though you have not got much experience in that field, you are confident enough to believe that you can carry out the role. Do you feel that you could be just as good as somebody who has already been in that role for a while? Let them know this.

Look at the skills you have. Highlight these, or experiences you may have had even in a voluntary role. Are the skills you have learnt transferrable? Tell them how your skills link to the advertised job role.

Why Have You Left Your Previous Job?

This is where a lot of people get stuck; they then blow the interview by offering too much information. Yes, you can give the interviewer too much. One thing which you should avoid is to bad mouth your previous employer. This shows that you are not loyal to the company. Explain that you want to seek new challenges or that you want to explore and achieve different opportunities.

There are also those that have been sacked or dismissed from their role. Each situation will bring a different circumstance. You probably won't be able to bring a great deal of positivity around your response. What I will say though is this, acknowledge and accept responsibility. You may need to explain a few facts first, but keep positive and make sure you say that it is all in your past and you are so motivated and determined to start fresh.

Have You Being Bullied?

The reason I have brought this into the book is that I have witnessed this first hand. Good people walk from their job because they feel it's the only way out. If this came up within an interview, you would need to watch your body language and tone of voice. This is because if you still feel resentment or bitterness this could spill over without you realising it. Would you want to employ somebody demonstrating these emotions within the interview? Show that you're a better person and that you have moved on.

Gaps In Your Career

There will be many of you that have gaps in your career, quite often these are explainable. I have met people who are trying to get back into employment after having long term sickness. This is explainable so don't be embarrassed.

It may be that you need to talk openly about it. But explain that you used the time spent at home as productively as possible.

If you have been out of work for some time can you explain what you have been doing to seek work? The interviewer needs to build up a picture of you, tell them you have been proactive in your search for employment. Have you put yourself onto training courses? Have you volunteered your services for free?

Throughout this section you will be asked a variety of questions. If you can answer these questions fully and give off fantastic positive body language and display passion then you will sail through every interview. This is where you will link all of the previous sections of this book. You are aware that you are up against a lot of other people; use this opportunity to make a positive impact.

The barriers you have will need to be faced and dealt with before an interview. Remember that the C.V has got you through the door, but you need to be the one that secures your future by delivering and responding competently. Take responsibility and do your homework.

I am now going to take you through some other interview questions. Try and link everything we have done, especially the Star Approach to responses.

Have a look on the next page at your interview questions and practice them. This is your 'mock interview'. Practice as though your life depends on it. Think about previous situations and try and relate every answer to a work example. If you have none or limited work experience then link each answer a situation you have been in. But you will really need the enthusiasm. They need to see potential in you.

ONE TO ONE INTERVIEW QUESTIONS

Read the questions below, some, if not all may seem daunting at first but believe me, once you know all of these then there should be no interview question that you get stuck on. After you have read the questions, score yourself on each question:

0 – cannot answer, 1 – can think of an answer after much thought, 2 – can fluently answer the question fully and make sure my tone of voice is enthusiastic and interesting.

Be honest; remember being 'self aware' is the key to a successful interview.

1. Tell me a bit about yourself.
2. What made you apply for this job?
3. What skills do you think you have for this post?
4. Can you tell me something that you are passionate about?
5. Give me an example of when team work made a difference.
6. How would your friends describe you in three words?
7. Can you describe a time when you have used your own initiative?
8. Where do you see yourself in five years time?
9. What do you know about our company?
10. What has been your greatest achievement to date?
11. Have you ever been in stressful situations? How did you deal with it?
12. I have interviewed ten people before you, why do you think I should choose you?
13. Would you be willing to work overtime but on the rare occasion you may not get paid for the first 20 minutes?

264

14. How do you think you could add value to the company?

15. What are your weaknesses?

16. What is your motivation in life?

17. What does team work mean to you?

18. Have you ever gone above and beyond for somebody?

19. What do you think of our 'values'?

20. Why do you think communication is important to an employer?

YOUR INTERVIEW SCORE AND ANALYSIS

What do you think of the above questions? Have you got your score added up? Take a look at the comments, take on board these comments and if practice is needed then practice. You must be brutally honest with yourself, if you cheat on the score, then your cheating yourself.

I cannot express enough just how important it is that the interviewer/s actually see some of your fantastic personality within the interview. This alongside excellent interview responses will soon have you in employment/promotion in no time.

You should be aiming to answer each question naturally, fluently, passionately with enthusiasm and a positive tone of voice within three seconds.

Analysis Score:

0 – 10	At least you're being honest. Make a note of which questions in particular you struggled with. Try and think of a situation from previous experiences (*not necessarily latest*), use the star approach. Really think about the question, once you have re-read it and understood it more, it will become easier to answer.
10 – 20	Well done, at least you're on your way there. You have recognised that improvements need to be made. Again, think of all previous situations, it doesn't always have to be work related but it helps if it is. Keep going over the ones that you are getting stuck with. Think of a situation related to the question and try and tailor the answer/s around that.
20 - 30	Fantastic. Why haven't you got a job? This score is really good, you are almost there. To make sure you keep answering the questions fluently etc, then know yourself even more. Take on board that what may be letting you down at the moment is the self doubt. Get rid of it because you have something to offer any employer.
30 - 40	Whatever! Sorry but I may be talking out of place here, but have you being totally honest. This score means that you feel that you can answer at least 10 questions fluently with enthusiasm and an interesting tone of voice. Again, I apologise but do a re-count. If you still feel you have the correct score then well done you. Get out there and get a job or promotion.

You may never be asked every single one of these questions within a one to one interview, but you may be over a period of different interviews. I have not put any answers down here because each individual response will be different.

266

What I do suggest is that you practice having a great response for all of them.

What *one* thing do you need to know before you can get maximum score on this task?

'Yourself'

ARE YOU OVER CONFIDENT (TO MASK YOUR DOUBTS)?

I ask this question for one good reason. Too many (me included) people and certainly some of the learners I have taught often say to me; *"I think I will do well in my first interview because I know my skills and what I can do."*

This is fab. But underneath the surface, on many occasions this statement has proven to be a cover up. This is where I say, *"To take ownership, be responsible."* By this I mean that it is okay to be weaker in many areas, especially within interviews, it's this weakness that we are working on. It takes a strong person to say: "Do *you know what; I don't feel ready for an interview because I don't know about myself yet."*

When I am told from a learner that they are confident and could sail through an interview I will always try and get them to come out of their **comfort zone** even further and prove it to me. I will do a one to one interview with them and let me tell you, I would not give half of them a job. Not on the first interview anyway. It is at this point that I need to be careful with what I say to them as I only intend to help them progress.

So do this with yourself. Ask yourself the following questions now you have tried answering the questions for the first time.

Ask yourself:

1. Would I give myself a job on the responses given?

2. Could I expand more on my answers?

3. Do I need to work on my communication?

4. Do I sound passionate and enthusiastic?

Again, be honest with yourself here. I strongly recommend that you now practice the one to one interview questions again and see how you score. You need to keep on doing this until you can say to yourself:

"That's it, I really cannot do anything more. I am answering the questions to the best of my ability and with passion and enthusiasm."

Look at the *interview reflection* exercise on the next page, when you have practiced your one to one interview for the last time. Then still be honest here and write down any points which you feel you need to work on.

OWN REFLECTION FROM ONE TO ONE INTERVIEW

Think about your one to one interview, how do you think you did?

In the space below, answer HONESTLY the questions.

Do you feel you answered all of the questions to the best of your ability?	
If not, how could you improve?	
What would you do differently if given the chance?	
Which question did you dislike?	
Which question do you feel let you down?	
Give your opinion overall how the interview went.	

By completing the above reflection exercise and writing down your thoughts will help you to further recognise and build on weaker areas.

I really want you to practice all of the questions I have gone through. I want you to improve on your first score, make a note of each score every time you go through the one to one questions.

269

I must stress though that it's brilliant that you can answer every interview question you come across, but can you do it with confidence, self belief, passion and enthusiasm?

Honestly, I know I bang on about this, but I just want you to realise that without this then your career prospects look dull.

What about trying a role play exercise with a friend/partner. You become the interviewer and ask all of the questions listed. How are they coming across to you? Do you think they look arrogant? Do you think they look competent? Why is this? Is it because they are aware of their own abilities? This task is similar to sharing good practice, take what you can and use it to your own advantage. Then swap places, let your friend interview you. Would they give you the job? If not, ask them why and build on this feedback. If they would, ask them why and take this on board when you go to your next interview.

6 EASY INTERVIEW QUESTIONS

FOR THOSE WHO ARE GETTING BACK INTO EMPLOYMENT

In this activity I have listed more *common* questions; I want you to think about. Use the space below to write down your thoughts. The purpose of this activity is mainly for those who have been out of work for quite some time.

Always have a response for your absence from employment.

1. I can see from your C.V that you have been out of work for a while, what have you been doing with your time?
2. Why did you leave your last employment/company?
3. What have you been doing to search for employment?
4. What transferrable skills have you got?
5. Did you get along with your previous bosses?
6. Do you feel that you are ready for getting back into work?

270

Here are some typical responses to the previous questions. These are what I have put down, obviously please don't lie and copy what I have put (especially if you haven't).

1. I can see from your C.V that you have been out of work for a while, what have you been doing with your time?

   While actively seeking employment I became a volunteer for The Charity Shop. I also completed adult literacy and adult numeracy. I would also use the internet for 5 hours each day searching for work.

2. Why did you leave your last employment/company?

   Due to redundancy I was asked to leave as my job role had changed and there were other people with more experience. I asked to be trained in other areas but they didn't have enough money to do this.

3. What have you been doing to search for employment?

   (Similar to question 1) but add in the fact that you go out of your way to introduce yourself to different companies to hand out your C.V. Offer your services for free for 2 hours per week so that employers know what type of worker you are.

4. What transferrable skills have you got?

   I feel that I have a huge amount of skills to transfer from my previous roles: team work, communication, problems solving, reliable, loyal, good time keeping.

5. Did you get along with your previous bosses?

    Yes, there was mutual respect shown. He knew I was hard working therefore would trust my judgements quite often.

6. Do you feel that you are ready for getting back into work?

    I feel more than ready; I just want the chance to prove what skills I have to offer the company. I have always shown loyalty in the past and would love to be given this chance to show it to you.

And there you have it! I have gone through some very hard and some quite easy questions. You have all of the answers; you have the knowledge to sail through the interview. My biggest piece of advice is that you need to be aware of yourself and what you have to offer a company.

Research the company and then ask yourself each question I have put down.

RECAP AND CONSOLIDATION

Once you have got to this stage then you are ready to go for that interview. You are ready to '*sell*' yourself, because you have something an employer wants. Just make sure you believe in yourself. What's the worst thing that could happen? Nothing. You will just keep on practicing and trying your best within each interview. I stated earlier at the beginning of the book that if you do want a job, then following all of these skills and using the knowledge you have learnt will certainly make you *stand out* from the crowd.

We have looked at the different types of interviews you could face and you now have the knowledge to be confident within these interviews. The biggest thing I want you to take away from this session is the fact that to have a successful interview you need to understand the following:

- Your skills, strengths and abilities
- Your self belief
- Why you deserve the job
- What can you offer
- How can you add value
- Your communication skills
- Your C.V
- The company
- How to use the STAR approach

For more interview questions you can always look on the internet, my main aim was to go through the most common ones I come across on a daily basis. If you practice giving a fantastic response to these questions then your interview should be fairly easy.

The hardest thing about an interview is if you don't know what you're about. I have sat in on many interviews and listened to people tell me about their interview horror stories. But one thing I will repeat is that you need to know your own skills and what you can offer the company.

I have met many people who have not worked for many years, and I do know that it can be a scary thought to sell yourself and your skills; especially if you feel that you have none. If this is you, go back to the start of this section and really dig deep into your ability and strengths. Think about what you have done with your time whilst been out of work.

Link every piece of advice I have given you and really believe that you have a value in any employment.

One last question:

Are you a plastic rose or are you a natural wild flower?

I would love you to shout at me and say:

"Do you know what Tracey, I started off as a plastic rose, but now I can see that I am becoming (or have become) a natural wild flower."

YOUR PERSONAL NOTE PAGE

In the space below, write down any thoughts, ideas and notes you feel will help you throughout the book.

_____

_____

_____

_____

_____

_____

_____

_____

_____

_____

_____

_____

_____

_____

_____

_____

_____

_____

NAUGHTY BUT NICE

I have mentioned in the book about a little secret to help you beat the *computer filter system* when applying for jobs and sending off your C.V. I cannot take the credit for this, but my old boss and employability co-ordinator, Ian Harrison told me this tip. I have mentioned *key words* and how the computer will scan your C.V and application form. Usually there is a rejection letter to follow or you are just ignored.

Well follow this tip:

1. Look at the key words on the advert. Write them down on a piece of paper.
2. Somewhere on the C.V/application form you are going to type out these words, maybe in a Header or Footer.
3. Once you have typed them out, make sure that your C.V is still aligned correctly.
4. Highlight the keywords you have just added.
5. Press the *font colour* on your toolbar and select white. It has washed the keywords out, but the computer will still pick them out. It's just the colour you have changed.
6. Go back and double check your C.V to make sure it is still perfect.
7. If you're unsure how to carry out this procedure, I am sure there will be a friend or family member to help you.

This tip is generally called '*White Wording*', basically your using a camouflage to get your C.V and application form noticed.

276

YOU'RE ALMOST THERE

Well done.

Hopefully, you will have gathered that I am passionate about what I do. I can relate to every single learner I have had the pleasure to meet along my teaching journey. And I promise you that by taking on board all of the advice, guidance and hopefully my support you will feel so confident in getting a job. So confident in having the self belief to push yourself forward for that promotion. To actually believe in yourself and your skills to say to your employers that enough is enough, you are handing in your notice because you have found another position, you have moved on to where you are going to be valued.

How do I know all of these skills work?

Because I have been there. I have lacked that self belief. I have doubted my strengths and skills. Don't get me wrong, some of you need to change the way in which you think. I did. You need to see a positive from every negative. I know it's hard, but again, it's what I do every day. I work hard and tell myself:

"There is no job I cannot do;
I just have not been trained up yet."

Tracey Morewood

I guarantee that every single person who I have had the pleasure to help gain employment or at least gain faith and self belief in themselves has always taken away *'skills for life'*.

This is down to the following:

- I fully believe in every learner, everyone has something to offer.
- They know that I have been in their shoes, shared the same experiences.
- My ability to motivate others
- Giving empathy and understanding to each individual.
- Knowing that each person is an individual and has different needs
- Display a huge amount of enthusiasm and passion within each session.
- I understand that they are not always lazy, just scared.
- I am funny, well I try to be. I am the only one who laughs though!

But I make sure everything is focused around the learner. All experiences within this book has been taken from my own and the experiences of the individuals who I have met on my own learning journey.

You will notice that I have not mentioned many books or websites to where I have taken the advice I have given from. Why do you think this is? Quite simply, it is all from my experience of what is actually needed. From what I firmly know has helped learners over the years. That this experience is from real examples, not exaggerated to impress you. Yes there are some fantastic web sites out there which can help – but again, I have written this book from my own thoughts and experiences. No crap, just straight to what has proven to be successful.

278

FINAL TIPS TO HELP YOU SUCCEED

Remember at the beginning I explained that to become successful you would need to go through a process. This process is not just for now or until you have read this book, it is for life. I hope you realise that this book can help you in the future, that you have gained *skills for life.*

Too many people think that to progress with gaining employment and/or changing careers is down to the C.V and interview. It isn't. It's through gaining self belief and confidence too. I do fully understand that people have far bigger barriers to overcome due to personal issues within their life. But now is the time to change your thought process. Believe that you deserve a chance; believe that you are an important person, just as important as the next person. It does not matter about your past. You still count.

USE YOUR TIME WISELY

How many of you feel that you could *'brush up'* on Literacy, Numeracy and ICT (computers) to name a few? My advice would be to go to your Local Community Centre or Job Centre and ask for advice on *free courses.* The above courses are usually free if seeking JSA and you can often study up to a level 3. Do what you can whilst you are looking for employment. But remember to list any gained qualifications on your C.V. This could make interviews even easier for you to explain the gap in work experience. Think about it, there are loads of courses out there, get it while it is free.

Even if you're not on JSA, many courses up to a level 2 will be free. Again, seek advice from an organisation such as: Colleges or *Next Steps* a great career advice centre (I get lots of help from their online web page with fantastic advice).

MY PERSONAL THANKS

To those who bought my book, I hope I have helped you. If not, then re-read it as I know that this process works. But you first must be open to allowing this process into your mind. Change the negative thoughts and take responsibility; your life and the opportunity of life is down to you and you only. Don't allow anyone to put you down or stop you from experiencing other opportunities in life.

To the learners I have met and inspired over the years, you too have inspired me. I found my passion in life, and that was educating others. Believing in others and seeing things from a different point of view. Through my years within offender learning, I met some truly marvellous people; may you jump through the hoops and get that second chance.

To friends and family who have supported me throughout my own problems – thank you. Thank you for your encouragement whilst I was doing this book.

Mr B for your advice and encouragement throughout. Bruno, for your understanding and amazing belief in me. No longer the plastic rose but the flower that grows.

To Steven Lever my book designer and Elaine Sharples for the typesetting. Thank you for your support throughout this new journey. You have made things a lot easier for me.

A GUIDE TO MY LINGO AND OTHER WORDS

Below I have listed some of the common words I have used throughout this book. These are *my* meanings and *my* interpretations. I have put it down straight forward and simple (a bit like me some would say).

Word	Meaning
Confidence	The belief that you are just as good as anyone else and can carry out a task competently
Affirmations	A really nice sentence that when read again can actually mean something.
Bang on	Keep repeating important issues/topics.
Barriers	A front which most people put on. Some are so used to it that they don't realise it's holding them back.
Biggin	To show off.
Body Language	What you are saying without opening your mouth.
Butt Kissing	Paying compliments to get somewhere in life.
C.V	Your *glossy brochure* which is the key to getting an interview. Curriculum Vitae.
Comfort Zone	A place where we feel comfy, stepping out and doing something different scares us.
Communication	One of the main skills an employer would like to see from present and future staff.
Cover Letter	A way to introduce yourself to the company, which is attached to your C.V

282

Word	Meaning
Dole or JSA	If you are not in employment and need to go to the Job Centre each week to get paid. Dole is what it was called in the 90's.
Employable	Having the work ethics, social skills and experience to do a good job. Qualifications are not always as important as employable skills.
Filter	An imaginable filter system stored in the subconscious mind, this will filter as a yes or no for the jobs.
Gipping	Retching, to feel sick.
Keywords	Words and expressions that stick out. That makes you more noticeable.
Man up	Be strong.
Probation Period	A period of time to which you will need to *prove* yourself to your employer (or they can just get rid of you).
Soft Skills	Closely related to employable skills, these focus more on self esteem, confidence, communicating, working with others, being self aware, problem solving.
Speculative Approach	Targeting company's for jobs even though there isn't one advertised.
Strengths	What makes you who you are.
Timeline	A continuous line of what you have been doing over the last 10 years.
Work Ethic	Your morals and opinions of your work,

A TINY BIT ABOUT ME.

After leaving school with no qualifications at all I went to work at Butlins in sunny Skeggy. Lasting only 2 weeks as I was homesick. When I got home I had the chance of a retail shop assistant vacancy. The interview was sat at the managers' house in the kitchen having a chat and I got the job. Yep, those where the days when it was more about who you knew rather than what you knew. I got the job and within 1 year, at the ripe old age of 19 I applied for the managers' position and again I got it. I stayed there for almost 10 years until I left to start a family. Up until this point I used to be embarrassed about my C.V as there was nothing to put on it. I then went into warehouse work and I became a permanent member of a Distribution Centre, only to be told the next day that this warehouse was changing how it ran and therefore we would be losing my job in the near future.

So what did I do? Did I sit around waiting to be made redundant? No. I took myself back to college to learn basic I.C.T. From there I enjoyed being back at college in my 30's and went onto other courses leading me to do a level 4 in ICT.

I applied for a role within Offender Learning, and went on to continue studying for my PGCE (Certificate in Education) and gained QTLS (Qualified Teacher Learning and Skills). I then realised that I needed a change in career and went into the Employability Sector for a Training Provider. Helping others achieve and succeed has always been a passion of mine and has kept me driven and focused.

But like I said earlier, I am not academically vocal and I worked hard to gain my qualifications. Okay, I am proud of what I have achieved. But, like anything else in this world, if you want something, you're going to have to go out and work for it.

The main point I just want to get across is that even if you leave school with NO QUALIFICATIONS it is not the end of the world. You can still achieve your goals. There is no barrier at all, except you and the nagging voice in your head.

Whilst writing this book, I too have been given news of redundancy. How do I feel? Scared to be honest in a way, but then I look at what I have to offer employers. I look at what I am about and know that any employer would be lucky to have me. I realise that sounds over confident but I believe in my skills and abilities to inspire others; after all I have a proven track record of this. I still want to progress, so instead of feeling sorry for myself, I have taken my own advice and I am ready for my next opportunity in life.

I must just say again that without meeting the learners along the way on my own journey, I can honestly say that I would not be in a position to write this book. I would not love what I do quite as much if it wasn't for the learner. And of course hopefully you will too be one of those learners who I have helped.

MY FINAL WORDS OF ENCOURAGEMENT

Remember these words:

Discover your potential and remain positive, your positive thinking will bring positive things.
Take one step at a time and make progress each day; regardless how small.
Start to live.
Sometimes things will go wrong, that black cloud will appear, have faith in yourself and you will find the strength to continue.
Above all, don't quit trying to reach the stars; you never know you may just reach the moon.

Thank you all

Tracey Morewood

287

USEFUL LINKS

BIBLIOGRAPHY

Feel the fear and do it anyway, Susan Jeffers, 2010
www.susanjeffers.com/home/bio.cfm

RESEARCH TOOLS

www.bbc.co.uk/news/10604117
www.sainsburys.co.uk/
www.boots.com
www.greggs.co.uk
www.coca-cola.co.uk
www.primark.co.uk
www.diy.com
www.marksandspencer.com
www.tgifridays.co.uk

USEFUL WEBSITES

You will find a wealth of information on the internet, you just need to search. I must just say that having looked at some information sites regarding the topic of this book, please be careful. Have they real life experience in this field? But the links below are what I would recommend and I have certainly used them to help my learners find work.

Take a look at these sites, some may be of use, especially when job searching. Remember it should take you roughly 1 hour to find a job, research it and apply.

It could take even longer depending on the application process.

www.direct.gov.uk	www.job-centre-vacancies.co.uk
www.indeed.co.uk	www.careeradviceonline.co.uk
www.jobsearch.co.uk	www.cv-library.co.uk
www.fish4.co.uk	www.careerjobsite.co.uk
www.monster.co.uk	www.reed.co.uk
www.needajob.co.uk	www.jobserve.com
www.totaljobs.com	www.google.co.uk/
www.dundee.ac.uk/careers	www.kent.ac.uk
www.retailchoice.com	www.jobs4warehousing.com
www.jobsite.co.uk	jobs.guardian.co.uk
www.jobstoday.co.uk	www.tes.co.uk/jobs

FUTURE DEVELOPMENTS

As I have mentioned within this book, it is important to set yourself goals, so what is my next goal? Another book. This time I am focussing on 'Interview Techniques'.

Hopefully I should have a website up and running, focussing on topics within the book. To take this a step further, I would also like to help *you* to develop your skills further. As I also mentioned earlier (in the C.V part) I am a qualified ICT lecturer, so I would like to do topics on basic ICT tools to help you create that all important C.V.
You may need to present a presentation to others 33using Microsoft PowerPoint. Maybe you just need to develop all aspects of using the Microsoft Package; again I can help you.

I would then like to offer webinars (a discussion or lesson directly over the internet). I have created a lot of resources to accompany my sessions; these will soon be available online for you to access.

My ultimate goal would be to open my own Training Company, helping those out of work become more employable. So you never know our paths my one day cross, I certainly hope so.

So once again, thank you so much for being my inspiration and good luck with your future employment. And as always I need to go on and on, but remember this:

"Don't allow anyone to put you down, don't be the victim anymore and believe that you have the skills to carry out any job; 'you just ain't been trained yet'. You're just as important as the next person; so make sure you keep telling yourself that."

Thank you and good luck with whatever you do in the future.

You will get that job or promotion, just believe in yourself and follow the guidance in this book.

You have identified and developed your skills; now put it all into practice. You have built the groundwork and foundation for your future – keep using this new found knowledge.

Tracey Morewood